Sweet

12 STEPS to CONGREGATIONAL TRANSFORMATION

A Practical Guide for Leaders

DAVID C. LAUBACH • FOREWORD BY THOMAS G. BANDY

JUDSON PRESS
PUBLISHERS SINCE 1824
VALLEY FORGE

12 Steps to Congregational Transformation: A Practical Guide for Leaders
© 2006 by Judson Press, Valley Forge, PA 19482-0851
All rights reserved.

The author and Judson Press have made every effort to trace the ownership of all quotes. In the event of a question arising from the use of a quote, we regret any error made and will be pleased to make the necessary correction in future printings and editions of this book.

Unless otherwise indicated, Bible quotations in this volume are from the New Revised Standard Bible, copyright 1989 by the Division of Christian Education of the National Council of Churches of Christ in the USA. Used by permission. Other translations cited are: Eugene H. Peterson, *The Message: The Bible in Contemporary Language* (Colorado Springs, Colo.: NavPress, 2002). The HOLY BIBLE, NEW INTERNATIONAL VERSION®. NIV®. Copyright © 1973, 1978, 1984 by International Bible Society. Used by permission of Zondervan Publishing House. All rights reserved (NIV). The Holy Bible, King James Version (KJV). The Revised Standard Version of the Bible, copyright 1946, 1952, 1971, and 1973 by the Division of Christian Education of the National Council of the Churches of Christ in the United States of America (RSV).

Cover and interior illustrations by Danny Ellison.

Library of Congress Cataloging-in-Publication Data

Laubach, David C.
12 steps to congregational transformation : a practical guide for leaders / David C. Laubach. — 1st ed.   p. cm.
Includes bibliographical references.
ISBN-13: 978-0-8170-1502-2 (pbk. : alk. paper) 1. Church renewal. 2. Christian leadership. I. Title. II. Title: Twelve steps to congregational transformation.
BV600.3.L385 2006
253—dc22   2006023193
Printed in the U.S.A.
First Edition, 2006.

CONTENTS

FOREWORD

I'd like to invite all pastors and lay leaders to step aside with me for a personal word. The first time I traveled to Australia, I bought three different guidebooks. Each one was a zillion pages long and covered every conceivable travel contingency, in every possible microculture, in every imaginable weather condition. I now know how to recognize snakes that I will never see and how to order food that I will never eat. Unfortunately, the guidebooks neglected to emphasize repeatedly that people drive and walk on the left, and I almost got killed at least a hundred times. True, it's a jungle out there and one day I will really appreciate the zillion pages in each guidebook, but at the beginning all I really (desperately!) needed were twelve steps to survive and thrive in another world.

The same is true for churches hoping to find their way in a new world. The multiplication of church-growth guidebooks are useful. One day you will need to explore all the nuances of culture and experiment with all the options for mission—and thank God for the zillion pages of advice. However, right now all you need is twelve steps to survive the trip and thrive in what will certainly feel like a foreign land. Believe me, it is a humbling experience.

Since I have you leaders to one side for a moment, this prompts me to share with you the one thing you absolutely must understand about modern culture and the established church. *People are incredibly selfish.* It's not just the "boomer" generation. It is nearly everybody, of all ages, races, and incomes. North America is a "me first" culture. Sure, people can be very generous with time and money for acute needs, but they are poor givers for chronic care.

The single most important thing leaders of change need to understand is that people are incredibly selfish.

After years of denominational and cross-denominational consulting for church growth, I am astonished at how many leaders are astonished at this. Somewhere in the midst of the twelve steps you will learn in this book, the sleepless pastor or lay leader suddenly realizes that people are *selfish*. Duh! *That's why they are resistant.* Churches magnetically attract selfish people because something inside compels them to seek healing, but make no mistake—most of those people inside (on your staff and board and membership rolls) are *still selfish people!* Even if God has healed them into temporary "unselfishness," they are remarkably prone to backslide into selfishness at the first signs of conflict or crisis.

Selfishness is not a state of being. It is a self-destructive habit, like smoking. Even after quitting, all it takes for the ex-smoker to start smoking again is for life to become suddenly stressful. Guess what? As a church leader you are about to make church life suddenly stressful, and it is going to send seemingly healthy church members right back into selfishness again. I've seen church members make it all the way through step 10 (as explained in this book), and suddenly start "smoking" again. The startled church leader pauses in midstride, thunderstruck, realizing that even after ten steps of transformation *people are still selfish!*

It is ironic that Dave Laubach begins this book describing the U-turn churches must make to "turn around and grow." I had a conversation with a church member who used exactly this metaphor. He was a veteran church member and retired school district superintendent. Every week he parked in the same parking space and sang his favorite music in the choir, wearing the gown that had his name sewn on the collar. His family sat in the same pew, and woe betides any newcomer who inadvertently sat there. He was a lifetime trustee and board member and never missed a meeting. This is what he said to me as a consultant to his church:

I really don't know where we have come from. I really don't care where we are now. I really don't want a vision. I just need the church to be a rock, an oasis, and open to celebrate my funeral. And Tom, I really, really, really don't need directions on how to get somewhere I don't want to go. How soon can you leave town?

Do you see what I mean? The same thing will be said to any church leader hoping to transform and turn around their church. It may not be articulated so well. It may be revealed by a raised eyebrow or an angry outburst, or by diminished giving or absenteeism, but it's there.

So, since I have you pastors and lay leaders aside for a moment, let me share with you the two things you need to know about breaking the habits of selfishness in the church.

First, you must break the hidden habit of selfishness that is within you. Yes, you are selfish too. We are all sinners, and you are no exception. I am amazed by how often I consult with a church that has made it through the first ten steps of transformation outlined in this book, but it is still not growing in spiritual depth and mission impact. It comes as a shock to the pastor and lay leaders to realize the problem is *them*. They were so busy freeing others from selfishness that they forgot to free themselves. How can you tell that you are still selfish?

- You are not a good coach, because you are unwilling to *be coached*. Your pride is in the way. You aren't able to admit mistakes, learn new things, and move beyond your own comfort zones.
- You are not able to be your very best. Your self-interest gets in the way. While Jesus says "follow me," you're worrying about career moves, a regular day off, and retirement plans.

6

So before you lead the church into steps 1–10, you may want to look ahead in this book and check out steps 11 and 12. It would be a shame to assemble an army, only to discover you are unprepared to lead it into battle.

Second, you must surrender everything to Christ. Ultimately, only God can liberate the sinner. Only Christ can heal you, your congregation, and North America from its profound habit of selfishness. You have to do more than pray. You have to make your life a prayer. Be ready for God's Spirit to intrude, upset, and change your church, your leadership, and your lifestyle. These days we hear a lot about any number of causes and precious relationships coming "first." But until Christ comes "first" the church will not grow. This is a hard challenge. I urge you to talk it over with your spouse and children before launching into the twelve steps of this book.

One of my own books connects the emerging faithful church with the earliest mission described in the New Testament. *Roadrunner* contrasts the "Body of Christ in Residence" with the "Body of Christ in Motion." I keep coming back to that metaphor again and again. In the end, this book is not just about twelve steps. It is about "stepping out." It is about walking with Christ into mission, and doing what the church is supposed to be about. Step, step, step, step … and keep going. It may take you five minutes or five years to move from one step described in this book to the next step. That's OK. Just don't stop. Keep going. God wants the church to be *in motion*.

—Thomas G. Bandy
August 2006

ACKNOWLEDGMENTS

Friends ask how long it has taken me to write this short book on congregational transformation. I sometimes answer, "Thirty-five years!" I am indebted to congregations I have served as pastor: the Aldenville and Clinton Center Baptist churches in Wayne County, Pennsylvania; the Mount Pleasant Baptist Church in Ambler, Pennsylvania; and the Cohansey Baptist Church in Roadstown, New Jersey. Each place of ministry has provided opportunities to grow and learn.

My twenty years with the national staff of the American Baptist Home Mission Society (National Ministries) have provided extraordinary opportunities to learn from great leaders of congregational transformation and from turnaround congregations. A special word of thanks to the executive director of National Ministries (NM), Dr. Aidsand F. Wright-Riggins, for blessing this writing project and providing support and time in this endeavor.

In the past decade, my perspective has been further enlarged because of my work with the Baptist World Alliance (BWA) and the privilege of learning from church leaders on every continent. Dr. Tony Cupit, recently retired director of the BWA evangelism and education department, opened many doors for me.

Thank you to my Judson Press editor, Rebecca Irwin-Diehl, for her excellent work in organizing and improving my first draft and in asking the hard questions that make my ideas clearer to readers. Thank you to my administrative assistant, Susan Bogle, for working with all the details of footnotes and versions. Thank you to Danny Ellison on his creative cartoon interpretations of the chapter themes. Thank you to the NM program staff who reviewed the Reflection/Action sections at the end of each chapter and made helpful suggestions and improvements.

Finally, once again I need to say a word of appreciation to my wife, Candace, for her grace and encouragement as I worked on yet another project that took time away from home and family.

INTRODUCTION

"Stagnant, stuck, and sterile!"[1] For many years, I borrowed this phrase from David Dethmers to describe congregations at an impasse and churches in decline. A definition of being stuck comes from Kenneth Halstead, who says a congregation is stuck when it "does not hear and respond to needs, is unable to foster a maturing faith in its members, and is unable to grow and adapt its structure to change." In a stuck congregation, members feel frustrated that the church is going nowhere or losing ground. "Its energy flow stagnates or drains away."[2] The alliteration, stagnant-stuck-sterile, sounds an alarm that inward-focused, maintenance-minded, and survival-mode congregations are not evangelizing, planting new churches, and reaching out to their communities in friendship and service.

Statistics tell us that in the United States more than 80 percent of churches have plateaued or are declining, and 50–75 churches close their doors every week.[3] My desire is to signal that many churches are in distress and that there ought to be urgency about recovering a faithful representation of the church. I deliberately use the vocabulary of transformation, which is the Latin form of the Greek word *metamorphosis,* to talk about change in the church. Transformation is that type of deep structural change that brings vitality, helps churches break free from unhealthy patterns, and produces fruit.

This book is for the leader who recognizes the challenging realities of the congregation today, has a vision for a healthier expression of Christ's church, and is looking for some help with the process of congregational renovation.

I feel compelled to say a word of qualification about the title of this book. As with any 12-step program, the journey toward transformation is much longer than twelve paces. Each step represents a stage in a process that will take some time. And while it is best and often necessary to start at the beginning, transforming a congregation is not like assembling a new bicycle. The steps are all critical, but different congregations in different situations will have different starting places in the process.

The similarity between *Twelve Steps to Congregational Transformation* and the twelve steps[4] of such recovery programs as Alcoholics Anonymous is not entirely contrived. The first step in recovery for alcoholics is to admit that they are powerless over alcohol and that their lives have become unmanageable. The first step for churches and leaders in recovery is to confess that we are powerless to change churches that have become unsustainable. It is only the greater power we name as Jesus who will restore us to a healthy life in the body. The journey toward personal and congregational transformation begins with the decision to turn our will and our lives over to the care of God.[5]

With each step I have included a biblical text and commentary that speak to the topic. After each step I have added questions and process for reflection as well as suggested actions. It will be in the conversation about change and the activity around renewal that transformation will happen.

The cartoons that introduce each step are not meant to trivialize the sacred business of continually renewing Christ's church. They are intended to make the point of that chapter visually and creatively. It will take all five senses (have you seen the Scratch and Sniff Bible?), all of our multiple intelligences, and our right and left brain to be partners with Christ, the church's founder in church renovation.

Husband: "Have you considered the possibility
that everyone *else* is lost?"

Make a U-Turn
Revelation 2:1-7

Christianity started out in Palestine as a fellowship. Then it moved to Greece and became a philosophy, then it went to Rome and became an institution, and then it went to Europe and became a government. Finally it came to America where we made it an enterprise.

—Richard Halverson,
while he was US Senate Chaplain

Things You Need to Know
1. Where have you been? Know your history.
2. Where are you now? Know your location.
3. How can you get to your destination? Ask for directions.

My rental car came with a navigational device. I entered my destination, then a satellite tracked my location and announced turns and exits. When I went off course, it advised me to make the first safe and legal U-turn. In the transformative ministry of congregational renewal, the metaphor of a safe and legal U-turn is incredibly apt. Renewal involves comparing your current location, your desired destination—and recognizing that a dramatic change in direction is needed.

In order to effect a congregational change in direction—to make that safe and legal U-turn—a church requires certain key pieces of information. You need to know where you have been, where you are now, where you want to be, and how you can get there. Don't be afraid to ask for directions!

Know Where You've Been

When it comes to congregational transformation, location is more than just a geographic reality. It encompasses organizational culture—where the church is positioned theologically, socially, emotionally. And you cannot have a clear sense of where you are now in those aspects of location until you discover how you got there. In other words, you can't appreciate where you are now until you learn where you have been.

A "cathedral church" in Los Angeles wanted some help with evangelism. As is my usual strategy, I began by asking them to share some of their congregational history. They told me the story of recent repairs following the Northwood earthquake of 1994. There had been structural damage to the sanctuary ceiling system, and when the plaster was removed during repairs, an unfinished skylight was discovered above the ceiling. That's when the church remembered the original architect's design had included a skylight, but because of financial constraints, it had been plastered over. A half century later, the congregation had finished the skylight and realized the vision of the builders.

I believed that this part of the church history represented a core congregational story—and it offered a powerful metaphor for their renewal. In a synchronous way, evangelism had been plastered over with lovely words about ecumenical, multicultural, community organizations that provided worthwhile services but lacked ministry partnerships and intentionality about congregational mission. The way forward was back, to the dream of those early visionaries—men and women who had sacrificed and built anew, who weren't tied to tradition or an old building but saw opportunity in that neighborhood and acted on that opportunity.

We began to ask, What was the blueprint of the founders for evangelism? The answer became transformative in the life of the members and of the community.

Know Where You Are

The maxim of real estate salespeople is "location, location, location." But as I mentioned already, location is not only about geography. A precondition to turning around is knowledge of your threefold location. Where on earth is your church in the twenty-first century—in terms of geography and demographics, of emotion, spirituality, and organizational culture, and of the position of your leadership?

Geography and Demographics

Ask questions of geography first. Where is your church building situated? Is it in an urban center, a suburban community, or a rural roadside? Is it an old "first church" with a cherished history or a new church plant? What are the limitations and opportunities of being planted in your particular neighborhood and community? Where do your members live in relation to the physical building?

Now ask questions related to demographics. Who are your members in relation to race, gender, age, profession or education, and socioeconomic status? Is the congregation diverse or homogenous in those categories? What is the median age and tenure of your members? How do they differ from residents of the immediate community? For your congregation and the community, ask about key transitions. Is there a shift in racial majority from white to Hispanic or African American to Korean? Is it a graying congregation with missing generations?

In light of all of these questions, how would you describe the church's organizational strengths and weaknesses when you think of resources and leadership? What direction and destination are suggested by these present realities?

Emotion, Spirituality, and Organizational Culture

When visitors describe a church as warm or cold, they are not usually referring to the heating and air conditioning. They are describing the collective behavior of church members, particularly as it relates to tendencies toward extroversion, invitations to intimacy, and overall congregational self-esteem. When you plot these qualities on a continuum, you are mapping the emotional location of a church. Awareness of a congregation's emotional location is more important than knowing the church's zip code, number of parking spaces, and census tract data. It will absolutely determine whether the church can make a U-turn.

Where is your congregation emotionally? How do members feel about one another, about the leaders, and about visitors or strangers? What is the overall mood of the congregation on a given Sunday? How does the church respond to a crisis, be it personal or organizational? How often has the congregation been struck with significant tragedy, conflict, or struggle?

What about the church's spiritual location? This question encompasses more than the bipartisan sociopolitical world in which we live—a world of blue states and red states, of conservatives and progressives and moderates. There are questions of spiritual maturity as well as of biblical interpretation and theological understanding. What does the church believe about God, about humanity, and about the world? And how do members handle differences of belief or discussion of so-called gray areas?

Then ask questions about the church's organizational culture. Author Robert Dale has plotted the development of a congregation on a curve that ascends from a dream, to beliefs, goals, and structure, and finally peaks with ministry. Then the curve descends from nostalgia, to questioning and polarization, and ultimately drops out.[1] Where along Dale's curve of congregational development might you locate your church? How does the organization respond to change, be it small or large scale? That last question is particularly key in assessing your location for the purpose of moving on in the process of renewal. There is no renewal without change.

Leadership

Finally, ask hard questions of yourself as a leader. Where are you in your education and skills? What is your experience, and what are your areas of competency? How would you characterize your spiritual vitality? In the church, at home, and in the community beyond, what is the state of your relational health? How connected are you to the people who live with you, work with you, or come into passing contact with you? What is your general attitude toward these people—and toward the ministry to which God has called you? What new direction is needed to reach God's destination for you as church leader?

A Case Study in Location

For many years I directed a lay renewal program called "Macedonia Ministries," named after the familiar text in Acts 16:9. One day a lay minister from New York called and said he had heard a "Macedonian call" from a Baptist pastor in England. Could we bring an American team to several congregations in southern England to help them in their renewal journey?

We arrived in Hampshire with a diverse team of laypersons, all eager to share our experiences and stories. We quickly discovered a disconcerting paradox. We had arrived at a Pentecostal British Baptist church! I didn't even know you could say these words all together in the same sentence. There had been a significant cultural misunderstanding between the Americans and the British. In the United States, renewal was a movement about actualizing the priesthood of all believers, which was only sometimes (and often controversially) tinged with the charismatic. In England, "renewal" meant something very different; it was profoundly charismatic. The miscommunication arose because neither the Americans nor the British understood the other's location. Once we were clear about location and concurred about a holistic destination that embraced passionate worship, vital relationship with God, and fellowship that provided support and accountability for living faith in daily life, then the Macedonia Ministries team members were able to work together with the British Baptists to effect the U-turn of congregational transformation in Hampshire.

Don't Forget to Ask for Directions

No matter what your current location—emotionally, spiritually, or organizationally—the path ahead is nearly always to return to the dream and beliefs and goals that led to ministry and to embrace them again or reimagine them. George Barna has repeatedly rehearsed the life cycle of different organizations from birth to development to maturity to decline and death.[2] Sociologists of religion teach that vital faith movements inevitably move toward becoming institutions—and institutionalization tends to sound the death knell of a vital faith. In fact, these sociologists observe that these once-vital faith movements experience renewal only when the elemental characteristics of their beginning break into their institutional life.

What does that mean for the Christian church? We often jest that when all else fails we should read the directions. For the church, this means reading about the early church in the New Testament. According to renowned author and founder of The Alban Institute, Loren Mead, today we live in a post-Christendom era that resembles the pre-Christendom apostolic era of the first century.[3] If we want to understand what ministry in post-Christendom looks like, we need to look back to the time before Constantine. Congregational transformation is a journey back to the future. The first step in this journey back to the future is to rediscover the biblical and historic roots of the church.

The Bible is not like most instruction manuals. In fact, it is a highly unusual user guide because it not only offers many models for how to assemble the church; it also includes among those models many examples of churches that are not assembled correctly. The flawed designs prove to be just as instructional, if not more so, than the ideal models.

I especially like to learn about being a church from the seven churches in Asia Minor, each of which received a letter from the Spirit via John's Revelation. The message from Jesus to the church at Ephesus sounds particularly contemporary and familiar. Here was a church that believed the right things and was hard at work doing good things. What could possibly be wrong with this church filled with good people, good works, and good doctrine? Revelation 2:4 reports that there was a serious defect in this church: "you have abandoned the love you had at first." And this was important and instructive enough to be shared with the other six churches in Asia Minor. The Ephesian Christians were admonished to "remember the height from which you have fallen" (J. Massyngberde Ford translation), to repent, and to do the works that issued from their first love.

All three verbs in Revelation 2:5 are important—remember, repent, do—and their sequence is also essential. Remembering—specifically, the original will of God for our life and our church—convicts us of the need to change direction, to go back to the future, to repent. And just as works proceed from faith, so doing proceeds from repentance. Repentance without action is an empty sentiment. And remembrance without repentance is merely nostalgia. Thus remembrance compels repentance, which in turn inspires action.

Remember

Remembering is a double-edged sword. It is not enough for the church to remember the "good old days" when faith and mission were vital and love was tangible. In the mid-1970s, I served a church in Ambler, Pennsylvania. The golden age of the church had been during the years before and following World War I, when the sanctuary was full and the church and pastor touched every segment of life in this suburban borough with the love of Jesus Christ. By the time I arrived as pastor, the church had become ingrown. The congregation was fond of looking backward and remembering the past—but in the wrong way.

I attempted to galvanize the congregation into acting on those memories—to seize the church's historical identity as one opportunity to spark renewal and transformation, not only in the congregation but also in the community nearby. Ultimately, however, I was unsuccessful in facilitating a transformative U-turn. Remembrance was merely nostalgia rather than a startling reminder of the personality of that earlier generation of believers who were risk takers and innovators, who extended themselves toward others and reached out into the community in creative and unlikely ways.

Repent

Our civil society values tolerance, accommodates incredible diversity and pluralism, and tends to perceive all individuals as victims. In this society, repentance is caricatured as an act practiced only by doomsayers. But the word *repent* is in the warning to the Ephesians, as well as in the warning to the churches at Pergamum, Thyatira, Sardis, and Laodicea, and so it seems safe to deem it relevant for the church in twenty-first century North America.

Repentance is not only an act of personal faith but also an act of communal faith. The Greek word for repentance, *metanoia*, is contemporary in its meaning: "to change one's mind" or "to change direction or turn around." Because of this literal meaning, the metaphor of renewal as a U-turn and the idea of congregational transformation producing "turnaround churches" become rich biblical images.

A classically liberal church in New Jersey offers a case study in this literal meaning of repentance. The congregation asked for some help with church growth. I started out by encouraging people to remember, to tell their congregational stories. I learned that the church had been among the first to integrate in the 1950s and organized against discriminatory real estate practices. Current events continued to be important discussion topics. But when I actively listened to the congregational stories, what I heard was a scarcity of language about God and an absence of language about the Holy Spirit. For that congregation seeking renewal, the way ahead was to repent—to turn around and reclaim the biblical and theological consensus that had informed the actions of their forebears. The way ahead was to turn back—even further back than their recent history to their first love.

Do

The third verb in Christ's exhortation to the Ephesian Christians was "do." For churches seeking renewal, the U-turn may involve doing fewer things but making a bigger difference. Remember Ecclesiastes 1:9: "What has been is what will be, and what has been done is what will be done; there is nothing new under the sun."

In my denomination, the American Baptist Churches in the USA, we have been working through a challenging shift in our organizational life. For years we reported to our board about our activity, about what we as staff were doing. Then the board began asking uncomfortable questions—not about how busy we were but about what difference we were making, not about how many attended an event but what effect the event had on participants. Now we are learning to tell the story of our effectiveness, not our activity—the story of how what we are doing is advancing our mission.

The emergent church movement[4] emphasizes doing the right thing, and in doing so, it echoes the concerns of Jesus about the Ephesian church. The Ephesians were given high marks for their orthodoxy (beliefs) but low marks in their orthopraxy (actions). In contrast, Brian McLaren writes that orthopraxy is the point of orthodoxy.[5]

We must act on our beliefs by acting out the love of Christ. As the quote from Richard Halverson suggests (p. 3), somewhere along the way Americans confused the church with a business. Boards and committees, bylaws and budgets, and meetings constrained by Robert's Rules of Order have multiplied like weeds. With 80 percent of our time and effort, what we do as the church is maintain the institution. What if we reversed the trend and released 80 percent of our members' gifts and ministries for use in the world?

A Concluding Word

Remembering, repenting, and doing are all powerful spiritual activities—and they all have elements of communal activity. To "re-member" is to put the members back together, often through the telling of congregational stories. James Hopewell has taught us, "Narratives, like sacraments, can be signs that do things."[6] Renewal at the congregational level requires repentance at that level also—a turnaround experience for the entire church.

Congregational discernment of purpose and mission is essential to the U-turn process. That discernment is not accomplished solely by the pastor reading a book or hosting a brainstorming session or appointing a task force (all of which can be helpful). The foundational activities of the church—evangelism and discipleship, including prayer and Bible study—must be done in community if the desired result is an emotionally-owned consensus about a direction—a broadly owned belief that God has spoken to the church for this time.

Remember why we are the church. The church is not an end in itself but a means to the ends of God's kingdom. The church must possess the right motivation (love of God), the right relationship (love for one another), and the right direction (love for the lost). It is easy to interpret the "first love" of Revelation as a call to rekindle the love we had for God when we were new Christians. James Moffatt takes us in a different direction with his translation: "remember the love you had for each other at first."

It is impossible to love God without loving one another (1 John

4:7-21). Jesus pressed that principle even further when he taught us to love our enemies. The world's verdict about the truth claims of Jesus and the Bible is influenced by whether people see love for one another in the church and love for neighbor in the lifestyle of Christians.

Reflection/Action

1. Discuss the letters to the seven churches of Asia Minor (Revelation 2–3). What are the positive characteristics of each church? What is Christ's complaint against each church? What is the U-turn needed? How are these churches and the needed U-turns similar to your church?

2. Form a renewal or vision team to study this book together. Begin by describing the present and preferred location of the congregation and leaders. Ask and answer the hard question of whether you are ready and willing to begin the journey of transformation.

3. Plan a one-day retreat or series of workshops to discern a scriptural text that speaks to your location and ministry opportunities. Plan for times of prayer and reflection on that text. Put feet under the text by rehearsing it with teaching and preaching and by weaving it into programs.

4. Interview key stakeholders in the life of the congregation. Look back over the past twenty-five years. What have been the significant stories of the congregation for each five-year period? What are the themes that emerge? What can you learn about how the congregation deals with change? Is there unfinished business from the past? Are there new dreams and possibilities for the future, or is the future an extension of the past?

5. Draw a timeline of the congregation from its founding date to a point five years from now. Ask leaders to draw the ups and downs of the church over this span of time. Make shorthand notes where there are peaks and valleys. Compare and discuss the various representations using the questions in the previous activity.

"Well, Pastor, the good news is there's just *one thing* we want you to do.
The bad news is that the one thing we want you to do…is change."

STEP 2

Choose to Change
1 Corinthians 12:27-31

We pray for them that are ministers of your word,
whose work it is, so far as a person is able, to draw
humankind to you. We pray that you will bless their
work, but that at the same time they themselves may
be drawn to you. Do not let them, in their zeal to
draw others to you, themselves neglect you.

—Søren Kierkegaard

What You Need to Choose
1. Choose to lead the change.
2. Choose to persevere in the process.
3. Choose to share in leadership.
4. Choose to lead in service.

We have all heard the joke that asks how many Baptists (insert the
name of your own denomination here) it takes to change a light
bulb. The punch line is "*Change?!*" Churches and leaders often
resist change because the familiar is comfortable. "Unchanging"
is not a word that describes the church institution, only the
church's message—but too many of us forget that fact. That's why
I often begin workshops on church change with a quiz about the
First Baptist Church in America founded in 1638 in Providence,
Rhode Island:

True or False[1]

1. There was a cross at the front of the sanctuary.
2. There were stained-glass windows.
3. There was organ music.
4. There were congregational hymns.
5. Children attended Sunday school.
6. Wine was used for Communion.
7. Scripture was read from the King James Version of the Bible.
8. Prayers were offered for missionaries.
9. Offering plates were used to receive tithes and offerings.
10. There was indoor plumbing.
11. The clergy were university-educated.
12. They met in a comfortable church building.

Except for the references to Communion wine (6) and clergy education (11), all of the statements are false, a point I emphasize to illustrate that change is inevitable. What's more, it is not necessary to look back to the seventeenth century to observe change. Consider your congregation. Is the congregation graying? Are you singing praise choruses with words projected on a screen? Does your church have a website? Do you have home discipleship groups? Is denominational loyalty ebbing? Have you sold the parsonage? Do worshippers clap and raise their hands? If you can answer yes to any of those questions, your church is further proof that change is continuous.

Jim Collins, the best-selling author of *Built to Last* and *From Good to Great*, asks us to picture an egg.[2] Day after day, it sits there. No one pays attention to it. Then one day, the shell cracks and out hops a chicken. All of a sudden, the major magazines and newspapers jump on the story: "Stunning Turnaround at Egg!" and "The Chick Who Led the Breakthrough at Egg!" From the outside, the story always reads like an overnight sensation—as if the egg had suddenly and radically altered itself into a chicken. Whether change comes too slowly to measure or too abruptly to accept, change is going to come. The challenge to us as leaders is how we will respond to that inevitable event.

Choose to Lead the Change

The experts agree: "We have seen very few turnarounds take place without replacing most of the present leaders. It is usually unwise to think that the same people who got the church into its current mess can lead it out of the mess."[3] "To turn around a church, a new pastor must be brought in to lead the revolution."[4] "Firing the minister or electing new lay leaders is a common approach [to revitalizing a church]."[5]

Having the right person in the right place with the right gifts is important. Indeed, even the secular business literature on the market (including those resources that have been "baptized" by church renovators) tells us that if you want to change the organization—in this case, the church—change the leaders. Therefore, the million-dollar question seems to be whether it is possible to change the leader, lay or clergy, without replacing the leader.

I believe it *is* possible for leaders to change—because God is in the business of changing people. And when people change, the church becomes transformed. I will discuss important principles of leading congregational change in Step 4, but if you hope to effect church transformation, the change in the congregation invariably begins with change in the leader—and that means you.

Now, a leader may change in the same way that many organizations change, strongly resisting and sometimes kicking and screaming, but as we have already established, change *will* come. Let me offer this challenge—and I encourage you to accept its invitation: Why not get in front of the change? Too often as leaders we end up trailing behind the change, trying to manage its effects and clean up the chaos that unplanned transition inevitably produces.

STEP 2

We end up in that position because we view change as a negative force, something that disrupts, distracts, and dismembers our congregations. The challenge is for us to change that perception of change itself. Learn to see it as a positive process, a divine work of re-creation and renewal. Embrace the words of the Lord: "Behold, I am doing a new thing!" Exchange your human anxiety about change for a supernatural anticipation of transformation—and communicate that peace and hope to your congregation.

A Connecticut pastor in a small town attributed the turnaround at his church to a single event. After seven years of satisfactory but not exceptional ministry, he made arrangements with the church for a sabbatical. He invested this time in personal growth and learning. He told me that the change in him was so significant that when he returned it was as if the church had called a new pastor. His preaching, leadership style, teaching, and missional approach were different. It turned out that not only did the church have a new pastor, but the pastor soon had a new congregation.

Choose to Persevere in the Process
Do not misunderstand what I mean by change, however. A study of denominational leadership shows a correlation between pastors who change churches frequently (and churches who change pastors frequently) and a lack of growth and health. Moving from one place to another produces spiritual and physical rootlessness—and without roots, nothing grows. Similarly, staying in one place but changing with the latest fads in ministry or the current trends in theology produces a comparable instability, personally and organizationally. Attempting transformation by trial-and-error theology and methodology is as self-defeating as frequently switching pastors or churches.

The only recipe for healthy growth is intentional, committed, and consistent change. That is true at the personal level as well as on the organizational plane—and keep in mind that the personal transformation must precede any congregational renewal. Take the time to discern the direction in which God is leading you. (In other words, know where you're going!) Then prayerfully and practically chart a course for yourself, and cast the vision and path to its realization to the congregation. Finally, set your feet on that path and do not swerve from it, even when confronted with adversity and setbacks. That is the commitment Paul demonstrated when he declared, "Do you not know that in a race the runners all compete, but only one receives the prize? Run in such a way that you may win it" (1 Corinthians 9:24).

A caution seems appropriate here: While personal change must precede or lead congregational change, leaders who get too far in front of their troops are often mistaken for the enemy. Effective leaders of change will bring others on board and have a team that supports one another in the stresses of leading change in the congregation.

The British biblical scholar Derek Tidball has written a wonderful book titled *Builders and Fools*.[6] In it, he describes eight biblical images for leadership, among which is that of pilot or navigator, taken from the list of ministry gifts in 1 Corinthians 12. The Greek word *kybernesis*, which in verse 28 has been translated as "governance," "administration," and more recently as "leadership," is used elsewhere in the New Testament in the ordinary sense of a pilot or sea captain (Acts 27:11; Revelation 18:17). Although it was the noun Greeks used to speak of the art of government, it was not administration in the modern sense of paper pushing or program management. Rather, it referred to steering the ship of state, involving the ability to chart a course and navigate through often troubled waters. The person gifted with this kind of leadership has both hands on the tiller and a close eye on the charts. It was an eminently appropriate metaphor in the first century, when the church was a ship in need of navigation through all sorts of hazards and weather conditions.[7]

Choose to Share in Leadership

Tidball further tells us that the pilot becomes a member of the crew, working as part of a larger team that depends heavily on that individual's leadership. That insight is profound. All too often, church leaders burn out because they try to chart the course, steer the ship, hoist the sails, and do the work of most of the crew.

I can testify to this dynamic. I am an adult child of an alcoholic (ACOA), and as the oldest child in my family, I learned the roles of rescuer and fixer. I also learned to work around dysfunctional systems—and *not* to ask for help. These patterns worked well during my early years as a pastor. I could handle all the visitations, lead the youth group, teach Sunday school, build the committee agendas, direct the Vacation Bible School, interface with the community, preside solo as worship leader, and even do carpentry and wiring for a church addition. I received praise and reward for following my ACOA script, but I failed to build congregational ownership, a leadership team, or a healthy, disciple-making church. During my recovery from this personally and ecclesiastically unhealthy behavior, I learned about the power of teams.

In the first year of my pastorate at a historic church in New Jersey, I was the senior high youth leader. I invested an enormous amount of time in building the youth group with considerable success—but I was exhausted and neglecting my own family. So, the second and third years in ministry, I hired seminary students to do the youth work. The fourth year I shifted to a team approach with even greater success. Four couples met weekly for dinner, planning, and support and led a graded youth program that included drama, music, Bible study, crafts, and recreation. The church paid for this team to attend training events and conferences and purchased youth ministry books and journals. Ultimately, we replicated this team approach in many other areas of church life. Boards and committees functioned as ministry teams that we sent to conferences and involved in outreach and event planning. As church members became part of teams that were places of learning, fellowship, and service, they grew as disciples and in commitment.

This is how I have come to understand 1 Corinthians 12:28 and the role of a leader as pilot. I did not abandon ship or try to do it all alone. I worked alongside the crew, "equipping saints for the work of ministry," helping all to hear their calling, and using my gift of leadership. That was Jesus' strategy also: to build an interdependent leadership team with diverse gifts. That is also how I understand the larger context of 1 Corinthians 12:27-31, which describes how the body of Christ depends on the gifts and ministries of all of its members.[8]

It is easy to nod your head when reading Paul's words about gifts and ministries, but it can be difficult to practice this biblical concept when certain gifts are involved. So-called reserved gifts are those traditionally associated with the ordained minister, such as shepherding, preaching, administration, and even some teaching. Congregations can be complicit in this fable of reserved gifts by insisting that only the pastor can do counseling and visitation, occupy the pulpit and lead worship, manage and supervise aspects of church work, and teach the catechism—after all, this is what he or she is paid to do. Pastors and other "professional" leaders may allow jealousy of others who excel in these ministries to block those members from fully using their God-given gifts.

One mark of a great leader is that he or she is not threatened by the gifts of others but intentionally seeks out those gifts that are missing or weak in his or her own ministry. If you want to be a change leader in your church, encourage and celebrate all the gifts God has bestowed on the congregation and create opportunities for persons to develop and use their gifts. In changing that aspect of your own leadership, you will discover that calling forth all the gifts of God's people will change the work of your ministry and result in true congregational transformation.

I remember a seminary professor teaching that the work of the pastor was to work himself or herself out of a job. The assumption was that when everyone is an effective minister, the professional minister would be unnecessary. I have discovered that working myself out of a job is never really an issue. There are always new persons to prepare for leadership, requiring a recasting of the vision of the church's purpose and mission, not as an end in and of itself but as the means to the end that is God's kingdom.

Choose to Lead in Service

Most church leaders are familiar with Robert Greenleaf's concept of the servant leader. It has been extremely influential in modern business management philosophy, and it finds easy support in the servant songs of Isaiah and in the life of Jesus, who said, "The Son of Man came not to be served but to serve" and "whoever wishes to be great among you must be your servant" (Matthew 20:28, 26).

However familiar the idea might be, I have found it is helpful to rehearse the story that influenced Greenleaf's concept—a story found in Hermann Hesse's *Journey to the East*. The central figure of the story's mythical journey is Leo, who accompanies a group of men as the servant who does menial chores while also sustaining them with his spirit and his song. Leo is a person of extraordinary presence, and all goes well while he journeys with the band. Suddenly Leo disappears, the group falls into disarray, and the journey is abandoned. They cannot make it without Leo the servant. After many years of wandering, one of the original group is taken into the order that sponsored the original journey. There he finds Leo and discovers that the person he knew as a servant was the titular head of the order, its guiding spirit and a great and noble leader.

Greenleaf writes, "But to me, this story clearly says that the great leader is seen as servant first, and that simple fact is the key to his greatness. Leo was actually the leader all of the time, but he was servant first because that was what he was, deep down inside. Leadership was bestowed on a man who was by nature a servant. It was something given, or assumed, that could be taken away. His servant nature was the real man, not bestowed, not assumed, and not to be taken away. He was servant first."[9] Here is a key to changing leaders: that they might learn to be servant of Christ's church—and lead through that service.

Let me be clear: The pastor as servant leader is not a doormat or the "hired help," as a layperson once told me. However, the image of the professional church leader is too rarely compatible with the servant as leader. A seminary student who was a gifted musician and a pastoral intern in a Baptist church was asked to sing for a worship service and refused because it wasn't in his contract. When I read about God's servants in the New Testament, I do not see a concern for status or professional boundaries. My experience of the servant leader is one who leads and teaches by example, a leader who rolls up his or her sleeves and labors alongside others, a player-coach who does not find any ministry too lowly or unfitting.

Consider one manifestation of such servant leadership. We presented an award to a pastor in West Virginia several years ago for significant ministry in a small community. When presented with the award and asked to explain the incredible change in a rural church, the pastor said simply that he had loved them into the change. No matter what, he had loved them unconditionally. When people saw that was the consistent style and direction of his leadership, they came aboard.

The "love chapter" in 1 Corinthians 13 applies to church leaders and congregations as much to individuals. Indeed, its concluding verses could be paraphrased,

> If I preach with the eloquence of James Forbes [insert the
> name of your favorite pulpiteer]; if I have a Ph.D. from an
> Ivy League school; if I can check off all of Richard Foster's

spiritual disciplines; if I am a martyr in sacrificing personal time, material possessions, and even my health, but do not have love—it doesn't mean a thing.

Love trumps everything else. That's why Jesus taught that the world will know we love him by how we love one another (John 13:35). If you love the people in your church, you will be patient and kind, bearing all things, believing all things, hoping all things, and enduring all things. There will be no place for envy, boastfulness, arrogance, rudeness, irritability, resentfulness, or insistence on your own way. This may be a road less traveled, but it is the only lifestyle that fosters lasting congregational vitality.

Reflection/Action

1. Discuss how you exercise the gift of leadership. How is it consistent with the word study in this chapter? How is it different?

2. Practice acts of servant leadership and reflect on your experiences and responses in a group. This is not a merit badge where one servant act completes the task, but a first step toward a lifestyle of servant leadership. Reflect on how a leadership style change will affect your ministry.

3. Know your spiritual gifts. Complete a spiritual gifts inventory such as *Discover Your Gifts and Learn How to Use Them* by Alvin J. Vander Griend. There are also many online versions of spiritual gifts inventories (see appendix, "Tool Kit"). Know how you compensate for missing gifts.

4. If you are ready to go deeper with some of the concepts in this chapter, try this activity with a trusted confidante. The four-pane Johari Window[10] teaches us that there is an open window where what we know and others know about us is common, a second where what we know about our self is hidden from others, a third where we are blind to what others know about us, and a fourth

unknown to our self and others. Enlarging the open window is always seen as desirable. With your close friend, risk exploring the second and third windows and be open to discovering strengths and weaknesses that are opportunities for personal change and growth as you prepare to lead congregational change. What steps are you willing to take toward personal change and growth?

5. For personal reflection: What script was written for you in your family of origin and by significant life events in adulthood? How does following this script help and hinder ministry and family relationships? Write a new script that reflects a changed behavior.

	Known to Self	Not Known to Self
Known to Others	OPEN	BLIND
Not Known to Others	HIDDEN	UNKNOWN

STEP 3

Check Yourself
1 Timothy 3:1-9

There is no distinction between office and person, professional and private life, clergy and laity, leader and follower.
—William M. Easum and Thomas G. Bandy,
Growing Spiritual Redwoods[1]

What You Need to Check
1. Check your balance in leadership function.
2. Check your personality preferences and strengths.
3. Check your motives and commitment.
4. Check your biblical job description.

It was fifteen minutes before I was to preach at a struggling church in Rochester. The pastor was panicked because I had not brought a robe and none of his robes fit me. Left with no options and without robes, we met next with the choir, where I was expecting prayer but heard a joke about an old man and green bananas. Later I learned that the organist was blocking all efforts at changes in worship that might attract new persons. I was unsurprised by that one person's success because the pastor did not evidence spiritual or relational health. Nor did he seem willing to do any of the hard work to effect change. A critical requirement for leaders who want to lead a movement toward church health is that they too be healthy. In order to be credible in leading change, you need to be a transformed transformer and a renewed renewer. You need to have firsthand experience of God's turnaround power before you dare teach others about it. Peter Scazzero, who has taught our denomination's church renewal classes, says, "As go the leaders, so goes the church."[2]

That point is so critical to the process of congregational transformation that, although we addressed it as part of Step 2, it needs to be a giant step of its own. In the last chapter, we talked about needing to choose to be the first to change. In this chapter, we want to look at some practical areas for assessing and implementing change in ourselves as leaders. Consider Step 3 a kind of spiritual examination comparable to your annual physical with your primary care physician.

Check Your Balance

One of the most helpful tools for understanding healthy church leadership is a simple grid in William M. Easum's *Sacred Cows Make Gourmet Burgers*.[3] In each quadrant of the grid, Easum supplies key words related to a particular aspect of leadership. In the faith quadrant, the focus is on personal spirituality and individual imitation of Jesus Christ in piety and integrity. In the mentor quadrant, the focus is disciple making and team building, teaching and equipping others for the long-term success of the ministry. In the vision quadrant, the focus is on allowing a big-picture understanding of what the ministry is called to

PERMISSION-GIVING LEADERS	
BALANCED LEADERS	
FAITH	MENTOR
Jesus Christ	Equipper
Excellence	Interns
Integrity	Long-Term View
Courage	Team Player
VISION	REALITY
Primary Tools	No Illusions
Compass	Responsible
Self-Defined	Detail
Shared	Care for Self

become; this understanding guides the leader and, through vision casting, the congregation. Finally, in the reality quadrant, the focus is grounded in the details of everyday life—of implementing the plan within practical limits and without delusions of grandeur.

If we are not grounded in faith (quadrant 1), we become career leaders. Ministry is only a profession; it is what we do rather than who we are becoming. If we are not mentoring others (quadrant 2), we are do-it-yourself leaders. We may be appreciated for our hard work, but we will create a pastor-dependent church and eventually burn out. If we lack vision (quadrant 3), we become helter-skelter leaders. We have no compass or map to guide our heart or our followers, and so we are susceptible to every wind of teaching or any passing trend. If we are not in touch with reality (quadrant 4), we are leaders dangerous to ourselves and to others. Our realities can be depressing, and the details of life can be deadly if not balanced with faith. I like Jim Collins's insistence on "confronting the brutal facts but never losing faith."[4]

Here is how I understand what Easum is teaching. To be a healthy, balanced leader, we need to function effectively in all four quadrants. When we are weak in even one area, we become less effective leaders. Neglecting any one quadrant is like removing a leg from a stool. Removing more quadrants makes a very unsteady leader, as the following examples from my travels show.

A Native American church leader had an incredible vision of creating a multicultural community and weaving American Indian culture and Christianity together in worship. His enthusiasm, authentic spirituality, and charisma attracted many people. But he failed to mentor or empower leaders, consistently dreamed of grandiose ministries that were unsustainable, and could not retain those he attracted. In his frustration, he blamed the church, the middle judicatory, and the national denomination for not adequately financing and supporting his vision. Leaders who have faith and vision but do not mentor their followers or ground their ministry in reality are frustrated leaders.

Leaders who lack faith and vision are dysfunctional leaders. I consulted with a church that had a pathologist who chaired their long-range planning committee. The medical doctor spent his days looking at the microscopic details of the present and had difficulty leaving this orientation behind when he showed up for committee meetings. As a result, the church committee dealt with neither long-range vision nor faith-based planning.

A leader whose strengths are faith and awareness of the realities of life may be personal chaplains to church members but not holistic and healthy leaders. We quickly learned that hard lesson when those whose strength limited them to personal chaplain work attempted new church planting. They attracted many needy people and grew quickly. The new members were hungry to receive pastoral care, nurture, and support. However, most were unable to contribute to the congregation—either financially or in leadership roles. Church attendance plateaued when the church planter reached a maximum counseling load.

Leaders who are strong in faith and mentoring and weak in vision and reality are described by Easum as touchy-feely leaders. This describes a pastor I knew whose deep and genuine personal piety, borne of significant life crises, inspired an enormous capacity to welcome people to his home and office, to help anyone who crossed his path, and to encourage others in developing their potential. Beyond the desire for the pastor to excel as a pastor, however, there was not any direction or vision for the church's future. Neither he nor the church grappled with the changing realities and challenges of the church, community, and culture.

Visionary leaders who attract and mentor followers of their visions without faith and without being planted in reality are what Easum calls crash-and-burn leaders. The horror of Jonestown demonstrates the most extreme form of this phenomenon, in which a leader with an aberrant faith developed a community around a "messianic" vision that was out of touch with reality. Another, less tragic example, is the "Christian" Ponzi scheme of a few years ago, which promised churches that their investments would be doubled through the generosity of anonymous donors. The hopes of churches that participated crashed and burned when the true motives of the CEO were exposed and the anonymous donors were proven to be fictitious. Crash-and-burn leaders inevitably take down their congregations with them.

Before you embark on a mission of congregational transformation, check your balance as a leader, and evaluate yourself periodically throughout the process. The sooner you identify the quadrant(s) that are lacking, the sooner you can get to work exercising those qualities to strengthen them, for your health and for the health of your congregation.

Check Your Personality

Similar principles of balanced function are at work when it comes to our natural personality types and emotional intelligence. If we are out of balance—functioning outside our usual preferences and strengths—then we will be less effective leaders. While there are many tools for assessing personality type, the instrument most commonly used and highly regarded is probably the Myers-Briggs Type Indicator (MBTI).

The MBTI teaches that each person has four preferences: Introversion (I) or Extroversion (E), Intuiting (N) or Sensing (S), Thinking (T) or Feeling (F), and Judging (J) or Perceiving (P). The first preference—introversion versus extroversion—deals with a person's favorite world. Extroverts are energized by interaction with the outside world of people and activity; introverts are energized by the inner world of thoughts and feelings.

The second preference—intuiting versus sensing—relates to how we process information. Sensates know what they experience with their five senses, while intuitives interpret information through a so-called sixth sense. Intuitives excel in the abstract; sensates are good with the concrete. Intuitives prefer the global view (the forest) and project far into the future; sensates focus on the details (the trees) and thrive in the here and now.

The third preference—thinking versus feeling—describes how we make decisions. Thinking types prefer rational and linear decision making. They make choices based on logic and consistency—according to what is fair. Feeling types factor people and special circumstances into their choices. They decide based on moral values and sensitivity to others' feelings.

The fourth and final preference—judging versus perceiving—relates to how we relate to the world outside ourselves. Judging types want to move quickly from point A to point Z, while perceiving types prefer the scenic route. Judging types like things swiftly decided and nailed down; perceiving types are comfortable with ambiguity and open-ended systems.

The MBTI theory posits that for each of these preference categories, one type is well developed, reliable, and favored (dominant). Our less preferred function (inferior) is immature and little used. The problem is that under stress our preferred functions don't work, and we regress to our less developed function. This is when we act childishly or out of character. To become more emotionally healthy, get to know your most inferior function. It will always be one of the interior functions: sensing or intuiting, thinking or feeling. Any of the popular books on MBTI[5] will help you identify your inferior function. M. Robert Mulholland Jr. writes persuasively of the need to develop our inferior function and sounds an alarm about the difficulties that Christian leaders face when they fail to develop it.[6] This can be as simple as someone who prefers the world of ideas and future forecasting (I) taking up a hobby that is sensing (S)—physically engaging and requiring attention to concrete details in the present. By reframing your weaknesses (inferior functions) as pportunities for growth and development, you can achieve improved balance and effectiveness as a leader of change and renewal.

Check Your Motives and Commitment

In 1988, I led a lay renewal team to Kodiak, Alaska. Our hosts arranged for a visit to the Russian Orthodox church and seminary in Kodiak, the oldest in the United States.[7] This was a new experience for most of us, and we had many questions to ask our seminarian-guide. We asked about the icons, the beautiful paintings that adorned the sanctuary, because we supposed that they are objects of worship. He explained that icons are windows. The gilded paintings of the biblical and Orthodox saints are windows to the eternal. We could look through the lives of these heroes and heroines of faith to see God. He observed that we ourselves are icons also. Lives, when lived in obedience to God, are windows through which others can see God's truth and love.

When we left that place, we took with us that powerful reminder that our lives are windows through which others see God. When ministry is just a job and not a calling, or when we are not walking in health and wholeness, it is harder for others to see God through us. How we care for our health—physically, emotionally, and spiritually—and how we handle stress or respond to loss is a witness to our faith.

Having said all that about the importance of a healthy leader, I want to offer what may seem like a contradiction. Church health can be built on weakness. For years I functioned effectively as the pastor of several churches without disclosing my own brokenness, weaknesses, struggles, and vulnerabilities. An intense two-week "calling and caring lab" at Princeton Theological Seminary with John Savage changed all of that.[8] I returned with a willingness to share my own stories of failure, humanity, and struggle and found that my relationships and ministry were strengthened. Peter Scazzero reports that a seismic shift occurred at the church where he served as pastor when he began to speak freely of mistakes, vulnerabilities, and failures; confessed openly his insecurities, disappointments, and shattered dreams; shared feelings of anger, jealousy, sadness, and despair; and even admitted "I don't know" at meetings with lay leaders and members. He quotes the familiar prayer of an unknown Confederate soldier to make his point.[9]

> I asked God for strength that I might achieve,
> I was made weak that I might learn humbly to obey. . . .
> I asked for power that I might have the praise of men,
> I was given weakness that I might feel the need of God.
> I asked for all things that I might enjoy life,
> I was given life that I might enjoy all things.
> I got nothing that I asked for, but everything I had hoped for.
> Almost despite myself,
> my unspoken prayers were answered. . . .

The difference between a good leader and a great leader is the leader's wisdom to attend to his or her health in the midst of the busiest schedule and most demanding workload and to be more effective because of it. "Level 5 Leadership" is Jim Collins's measure for great leaders who have a paradoxical blend of humility and professional will.[10] Great leaders are ambitious for the cause, the movement, and the mission—not for themselves. Collins writes that these leaders are responsible for ensuring that the right decisions are made, even if they don't have the executive power to make those decisions unilaterally and even if those decisions would not win a popular vote. In the social sector, which includes churches, the keys to leadership are the art of persuasion, a demonstration of shared interests, and the people's confidence that the leader is motivated by the greatness of the work and not self-interest.[11]

The history of Christianity is filled with millions of faithful servants whose names are known only to a few or who will be forgotten by future generations. Ask yourself who has been the most important and influential person in your life. Now consider for whom you are an important influence. These are the appropriate questions. God always knows the chain of influence that continues the spread of the gospel. Jesus promised the faithful that he would "confess your name before my father and before his angels" (Revelation 3:5).

Check Your Biblical Job Description

There are countless examples of leadership in the Bible. I have been drawn to a list of leadership characteristics in the Pastoral Epistles. The description of bishops and deacons in 1 Timothy 3:1-9 fits my understanding of leadership in the church—perhaps not in the specifics but in principle.

The roles of overseer (bishop) and minister/servant (deacon) are, by any other name, the roles of church leaders. The spiritual and relational vitality that is the driving force in congregational change[12] is in this text. Bishops and deacons are to be sensible and serious— a description that need not exclude a sense of humor and appreciation for the ridiculous. Leaders are expected to be gentle and not quarrelsome, temperate (or self-controlled) and not conceited, not double-tongued but blameless; they must "hold fast to the mystery of the faith with a clear conscience" (1 Timothy 3:9). Twice the writer to Timothy speaks of the leader's relationship to money: the bishop or deacon must not be a lover of money or greedy for gain. Relational vitality is also prominent in the passage. Leaders are to be hospitable, above reproach, and well thought of by outsiders. They should have a good relationship with their spouse and provide leadership in their home as well as outside of it. And not least of all, the bishop is to be an apt teacher. This is the mentor role: the leader instructs other leaders and equips them for the work of ministry.

Most of us conscientiously visit doctors and dentists for check-ups, and we work to correct unhealthy conditions. I challenge you to visit Dr. Timothy for a ministry-fitness checkup and evaluate your leadership health. Look at each word in the text, and score yourself on items such as temperance, hospitality, gentleness, management, and reputation. What prescriptions are called for to improve your health?

A Final Check

Speaking of check-ups. . . ! Although physical health has not been the primary focus of this chapter, our physical fitness often mirrors our emotional and spiritual health—and it is important that we have the physical stamina to lead organizational change. My annual physical includes an examination and routine tests, as well as a discussion about diet, exercise, and stress management. It is important to know your vital signs such as blood pressure, cholesterol, and, for males, PSA numbers. It is equally important to change behaviors and make lifestyle choices that improve your health. A health checkup for church leaders is similar. It is important to chart issues of self-awareness, balance, temperament, and emotional competency. It is equally important that the checkup motivate us to exercise spiritually, to monitor our emotions, to develop our personality, and thereby to change our leadership style.

Reflection/Action

1. Create a chart from the characteristics in 1 Timothy 3 and rate yourself in each of the areas. In your personal Bible study time, write out the observable behaviors associated with each characteristic.

2. Who are the persons you have known that you consider to be exemplary leaders? What did you observe about them that made them effective leaders?

3. Review Easum's grid of faith, vision, mentor, reality (p. 40). Which is your strength? Which is your Achilles heel? What is needed to strengthen the area of weakness?

4. Discover the Myers-Briggs personality type of church leaders. If a professional inventory is not possible, there is a self-administered variation in *Please Understand Me*.[13] Note your "inferior functions" or "least preferred" preferences. What activity might strengthen your underdeveloped personality preference? Where are the clusters of strength and gaps among leaders as a group?

5. Brainstorm and then rank what steps could be taken to broaden and deepen discipleship ministries in the congregation and among leaders. What one or two things are high leverage and could be implemented in the near future?

"Of course I knew there would be stress with this job. I just didn't
think the stress would be so stressful."

STEP 4

Assess Your Congregation
Matthew 13:1-9

Indeed, in the present climate of mistrust of institutions, many people who yearn for a more meaningful and fulfilling life would regard the church as an unlikely place to go for guidance.

—Hugh Mackay[1]

What You Need to Expect
1. Expect the stress.
2. Expect the conflict.
3. Expect the benefits.
4. Expect the mixed results.

Many of us live, work, and even play in environments that are climate-controlled all year round—heat in the winter, air conditioning and fans in the summer, and thermostats to adjust as desired in spring and fall. Of course, there are times when nature defies our attempts at control. It is always a mistake to underestimate the power of changes in climate—and to overestimate our ability to control such changes.

What is true in meteorology is also true in ecclesiology. Just as a city or region of a country has a climate, so do individual congregations within Christ's church. And just as changes in regional climate cause stress, crisis, and even chaos in a community, so will change dramatically affect the climate in a congregation.

STEP 4

Expect the Stress

Let me reiterate that point: *All* congregational change raises the organizational temperature. The heat is experienced in conflict and stress. Consider, for example, the renewal Jesus sought to introduce to the first-century temple and synagogues (see Matthew 22:29; 23:3, 15-16; 24:2). The result of Christ's transformative leadership was that "the chief priests and the elders of the people . . . conspired to arrest Jesus by stealth and kill him" (26:3-4). To say that Jesus' efforts caused stress is a vast understatement!

I asked the pastor of a successful turnaround church on Cape Cod to describe the process of change. The most memorable thing he said was that the process was extremely stressful. Even when the transition is viewed as beneficial, change is always stressful, consuming vast resources of time, energy, and talent. In many cases, even the stress of good change becomes a heavy burden, jeopardizing a pastor's physical, emotional, spiritual, and relational health. That risk is even more dramatic when the change is met with resistance.

As a leader, expect the stress and prepare for it. Establish a strong support system—one that is *not* a committee of church members but of persons outside the congregation. In all of our national transformation initiatives, we have built peer support groups into the program design. Often these groups are facilitated by a mentor or coach. They meet a minimum of once every other month. These peer groups meet to address a variety of critical needs: to pray, share lessons learned, collaborate, problem solve, plan, coach, provide accountability, and celebrate.

Change is stressful; there's no escaping that fact. Expect the stress, and plan for it, personally and organizationally. That is a far better approach than risking your health or the health of your family, and it is the only way to ensure your chances of completing the renewal process you have started.

50

Expect the Conflict

When the obstacle to change and transformation is an individual or family, the stress of confronting that obstacle can be great. All too often, leaders will allow a single dissatisfied church member to veto hopes and sabotage plans for positive change. Consider the example of a suburban Pennsylvania church that called a pastor to lead renewal. However, when the pastor attempted to make changes, he hit a deep pothole. One family issued an ultimatum: the pastor's initiatives had to go or they would leave. The church conceded, unwilling to risk losing this longtime member and family. Regrettably, the church ended up losing a lot more. In a short time, the pastor resigned, and most of the search committee members left the church.

Hartford Seminary's David Roozen has observed that denominational leaders think of local congregations as "purposive" while local congregations tend to be "communal" organizations.[2] That is, denominations believe that congregations exist to encourage and equip members for service and witness in the world. In contrast, many local churches prioritize their life together in community over making a difference in their larger context. Whenever the communal priority of internal relationships is challenged by a denomination's assertion of missional purpose, the potential for conflict develops.

A system experiencing stress inevitably transmits that stress to its leaders—and that stress, which is experienced individually and communally, almost inevitably gives rise to conflict. Thus, a massive obstacle to transformation becomes a failure to recognize that such stress and conflict are a normal part of the change process. The pastor, as a primary congregational leader, is often the lightning rod, attracting criticism and complaints. In much the same way that stress should be expected and planned for, conflict also should be anticipated, led, and managed.

There seems to be something in the DNA of many pastors that shuns conflict, and this avoidance only adds to the leader's stress

51

level. It is not surprising that Roy Oswald and Otto Kroeger, in *Personality Type and Religious Leadership*, report that the most frequently occurring Myers-Briggs type for clergy is ENFJ. This observation is significant because that type preference prefers harmony. Generally speaking, iNtuitive Feeling (NF) types "do not do well with difference and disagreement. They have difficulty seeing the useful side of conflict."[3]

That generalization rings true for me. My Myers-Briggs personality preference is NF, and as I mentioned before, I am an ACOA. Thus I was wired by nature and nurture to avoid conflict. As an adult, however, I discovered that avoiding conflict always seemed to get me into trouble. Now I am a recovering conflict-avoider. Here is a story from my recovery journey.

The yoked parish I served while in seminary not only had two buildings and two worship services but two sets of church officers, including two treasurers. The two churches jointly owned stock, and the two treasurers disagreed over where the dividend checks should be mailed. At that time, I was not far enough along in my recovery to confront in a direct and blunt way what was a long history of interpersonal conflict between these two officers. That notwithstanding, I found an NF way to confront the ostensibly uncooperative treasurer. I drove to his farm and described the standoff as I understood it. Then I asked him to help me figure out a solution to this recurring problem. He did.

I found an approach that satisfied my NF preference for harmony without compromising the health of the church or my health. I dealt as directly and immediately as possible with the conflict, so that the stress did not become burdensome and the crisis did not worsen.

Expect the Benefits

Contrary to the typical NF perception, there *is* a useful and healthy side to conflict—a beneficial effect that can be discovered only if we resist the urge to quit when resistance to change surfaces, or, conversely, the compulsion to drive ahead to implement change regardless of the casualties. If we will overcome our typical aversion to conflict in general and put aside past experiences with unhealthy conflict, we can come to recognize that conflict is necessary for successful problem solving and effective interpersonal relationships. That single insight may make all of the difference in leading a transformation process.

People have a tendency to focus on the differences experienced with others rather than focusing on the beliefs and goals they have in common. One of the basic principles of conflict management is to step back from the immediate disagreement and find the overarching areas of agreement—to recognize that we have common goals and purposes. Our disagreement is usually about methods. Once the larger goals are clear and the discussions are about ideas rather than persons, we can differ and debate with healthy outcomes. Disagreement often results in better assessment of options, better decisions, and a better direction.

Conflict can be healthy, and conflict avoidance can be unhealthy. In *The Four Obsessions of an Extraordinary Executive*, Patrick Lencioni describes an extraordinary executive, Rich O'Connor, and his management team.[4] A former employee characterized the company's culture to a competitor: "They argue constantly." All parties were comfortable stating their position on important issues and arguing the merits of their perspective. There was no personal dislike of one another, just heated debate about issues people care deeply about. Better decisions, mutual respect, and (usually) consensus were the outcome of this work style. O'Connor has created a climate in which healthy conflict is positive and a cohesive leadership team is able to argue like brothers and sisters.

Remember and remind others that change is a constant—and many times it brings about blessings and rewards. Whenever possible, reconnect the idea of current congregational transition with the history of the church and significant episodes of past change.

Look for principles in the nostalgic stories about the good old days and find present-day and future applications. For example, a declining New Jersey church bragged that in the 1960s they challenged local real estate agents whose practices maintained racial segregation. They had lost some members but gained others committed to fairness and justice. The change the congregation had implemented decades ago was a change for good. The challenge was to get the people to embrace current change as a good thing as well—as an opportunity for spiritual and numerical growth, clarification of vision, and advancement of the kingdom.

Expect the Mixed Results

Even when the net results of a congregational change are beneficial, the transition will still generate some stress and conflict. I cochaired a church renovation committee that replaced a worn Carnegie pipe organ with a new digital organ. We carefully researched the cost of restoration, replacement with a modest new pipe organ, and replacement with a quality digital organ. We discussed biblical issues of stewardship and the role of music in worship. We developed a spiritual renovation emphasis to parallel the organ decision (which was part of a larger sanctuary renovation). In sum, we used all the change management skills we knew to get everyone to support this decision—and we still lost a significant church family over the emotionally charged change.

Those who lead change should have their eyes wide open to the dynamics of change and the cost of change and expect mixed results. That is one lesson to be gleaned from Jesus' parable of the sower (Matthew 13:1-9). We know the familiar images: seeds devoured by birds, scorched by the sun, choked by thorns, and those that produced a harvest. It is easy to see an analogy with congregational transformation. Congregational transformation is the sowing of seeds of renewal, in which the harvest may vary greatly depending on the soil and a host of other factors, including the amount of sun and rain the season brings.

In my second pastorate, I persuaded the congregation to host a three-day training event in Family Clusters, an intergenerational family development model.[5] Members of our church and neighboring churches attended. Representatives from community social agencies also participated. Ultimately, however, all of our efforts to launch a Family Cluster program failed. The seeds of this renewal strategy did not fall on good ground, and the sprouts withered. Then, several years later, in my third pastorate, I introduced the concept of Family Clusters anew, and soon we had the support of the church and interested families who were planning and leading weekly intergenerational meetings. The same seed fell on good soil this time and brought forth fruit.

As leaders, we have to expect mixed results when we sow seeds of congregational change. The question should be, How can we cooperate with God so that more of the seeds of renewal bring forth grain thirty-, sixty-, and one hundred-fold? The rural church I served while in seminary had many farmers who shared their abundance. One farmer told us that he always planted enough sweet corn for his family as well as for the deer and raccoons *and* the pastor's family. Perhaps we need to plant extra seeds to allow for the deer and raccoons (comparable to the parable's birds, rocky soil, and thorns). Or maybe we need to plant so many prayers, ideas, and strategies that some eventually fall on good soil.

Consider the garden that is your church. Do you need to get rid of the "birds" in your church that eat the seeds before they can take root? Do you need better plows and fertilizer (e.g., newer technology and larger budget)? Might you need to pull up the thorns—all the nonessential things that choke out what is important? You should also remember Jesus' warning in the parable of the wheat and weeds about not separating them until the harvest (Matthew 13:24-30).

Conflict in the church has a chilling effect on mission and evangelism. It is difficult to foster health and growth in congregations when we are polarized and our energy is diverted from mission to intrafamily conflict. This is hard soil in which to grow seeds. Or to return to our original metaphor, seeds do not sprout when the temperature is cold, and seedlings do not survive when there is frost. As leaders, we must pay attention to the climate when we are planting seeds of renewal. Discern the season for change by asking these questions:

1. How ready is the congregation for a journey of transformation?
2. What are positive ways you have seen change managed in your congregation?
3. What significant stressors might limit your capacity to deal with the added stresses of transformational change?
4. What patterns of conflict have you observed among members?
5. As leader, how do you cope with stress and conflict?
6. How would you characterize the climate of your church? How will those conditions affect your turnaround seeds?

One More Look at the Parable

Of course, as analogous as the parable of the sower is for contemporary congregational transformation, an honest exegesis demands that we keep reading and see that Jesus identifies the seeds as the "word of the kingdom" (Matthew 13:19). Renewal and transformation came to people and communities because of the proclamation of the Good News of the kingdom of God. The birds are not deacons and trustees, nor Pharisees and Sadducees, but the evil one (v. 19). Jesus' parable illustrates that there is always spiritual warfare when we seek to grow spiritually and strengthen Christ's church. *Satan* is rightly translated "adversary"—and in this case, what he opposes is the development of healthy churches. Jesus tells the disciples that the point of the rocky soil and shallow roots is that we must be able to withstand tribulation and persecution and not fall away (v. 21). There will be internal and external challenges that will require a leader who is spiritually rooted deep. The thorns are more than the busy church schedule; they are the distractions of the world (v. 22). Eugene Peterson paraphrases this: "The seed cast in the weeds is the person who hears the kingdom news, but weeds of worry and illusions about getting more and wanting everything under the sun strangle what was heard and nothing comes of it."

Finally, as leaders of congregational transformation, remember Paul's words in 1 Corinthians 3:5-7: "What then is Apollos? What is Paul? Servants through whom you came to believe, as the Lord assigned to each. I planted, Apollos watered, but God gave the growth. So neither the one who plants nor the one who waters is anything, but only God who gives the growth."

Reflection/Action

1. What happens to seeds that are sown in the life and ministry of your congregation? What are the soil and climate conditions? What are the environmental threats?

2. How do Roozen's "purposive" and "communal" priorities balance or conflict in your experience? How well does your congregation align with its denominational partners, and how do you as a leader deal with points of disagreement?

3. Describe your experience of healthy versus unhealthy conflict. When have you stopped a change process because you valued harmony and were unwilling to confront the obstacles to change?

4. How do you, as the lightning rod for stress and conflict, get through the stresses of managing change? What kind of support system do you have? How might you build such a system if it is not in place or needs to be rebuilt?

"Okay, can you tell me again why you think
something might be wrong with the foundation?"

Convert the Church
Ezekiel 37:1-14

The church does not have a mission, it is God's mission and the Holy Spirit is missionary. The question is whether the mission of God has a church and whether the missionary activity of the Holy Spirit has an ecclesiastical partner and place to bring God's work to fulfillment.

—Attributed to Lesslie Newbigin

What You Need to Do

1. Study the Scriptures.
2. Serve other people.
3. Support the body of Christ.

A pastor called one of our offices and asked our director of congregational transformation about renewal. The pastor wanted a program, a resource, a guest speaker, a workshop, a quick fix. He was stuck and floundering for help in getting unstuck. The director asked if the minister had been praying about this—not the kind of prayer that is routinized and clichéd in worship or meetings but a discipline of prayer, a concert of prayer. Prayer walks in the church and community, focused prayer, vigils of prayer, and prayer warriors. Serious, searching prayer. It is not unusual for my colleagues and me to receive telephone calls asking for help in turning around an unhealthy church. Usually the caller is looking for resources, tools, solutions, fixes. Dallas Willard once held an audience on the edge of their seats as he promised to tell them the secret to church renewal: "Do the right thing [pause] all the time." What is the right thing? Your church *can* grow. I can almost guarantee it. You can tinker with the machinery to improve the attractiveness and awareness of church activities and to increase attendance, participation, and giving. A church in Marin County, California, does a living Nativity that requires tons of trucked-in sand. A church in Los Angeles has a Coke machine in the sanctuary. A church near San Diego has lawn chairs, Starbucks, Danish, and very casual dress. But growth does not necessarily translate into true renewal.

I am convinced now that, as required by 12-step programs, a congregation must come to a place where it acknowledges that it is helpless without the power Jesus gave his church at Pentecost. Ben Johnson, author of 95 *Theses for the Church*, seems to agree. He has observed that while most congregations are in dire need of transformation and revitalization, that process begins only with a recovery of a sense of the presence of God.[1] The power of the Holy Spirit, the presence of God . . . these enable one to effect real change. The question becomes How can a church tap into that power and presence? It is time to talk about winning Christians to a living faith and converting the church to become the body of Christ.

The respected author of *Celebration of Discipline*, Richard Foster, makes a compelling argument that the best way to recover that sense of God's presence, to renew one's intimacy with God, is through practicing the spiritual disciplines. He writes about the inward disciplines of meditation, prayer, fasting, study; the outward disciplines of simplicity, solitude, submission, and service; and of the corporate disciplines of confession, worship, guidance, and celebration.[2] Let us consider each of those groups in turn, and consider how the disciplines might teach us how to do the right thing—the real right thing—all the time.

Study: The Inward Disciplines

Study is the focused reading of the words of Scripture—its history, its context, its genre and place in the biblical canon—and so it may also involve study of other biblical tools that aid in comprehending the ancient culture, languages, and texts. In contrast, meditation is focused reflection on the meaning of a scriptural text; it might also involve contemplation of a particular quality or work of God. Prayer is a discipline that encompasses a variety of approaches to divine-human communication—from thanksgiving to intercession to petition. Fasting is a discipline that requires self-sacrifice for the purpose of focusing all senses and aspects of our being on God. Note that it may or may not involve abstaining from all food; it could be a decision to give up a favorite substance (sweets or caffeine), forego a preferred form of entertainment (television or movies), or refrain from certain personal luxuries (manicures or e-Bay).

Each of these inward disciplines is intended to cultivate personal intimacy with God. In a very real sense, they teach us how to obey the final part of Micah 6:8: "He has told you, O mortal, what is good; and what does the LORD require of you but to do justice, and to love kindness, and to walk humbly with your God?"

Converted churches that practice these inward disciplines will "hear the word of the Lord." They will not confuse activity and busyness with spiritual health. Converted churches will welcome the presence and work of the Holy Spirit because it is the breath that animates and gives life. They will be open to new life coming from the outside in surprising and unexpected ways. They will discover a new intimacy with God, which will in turn inspire their witness in the world.

Serve: The Outward Disciplines

Chief Slow Turtle, a Wampanoag from Mashpee, Massachusetts, and a descendant of Massasoit and the Indians who shared the first Thanksgiving with the Pilgrims, had been a longtime choir member and deacon of the Baptist church. His positive feelings about church soured, however, when local congregations took sides with a prominent family in a land dispute with the tribe. On his deathbed, Chief Slow Turtle recorded a message to be played at his funeral, a funeral attended by nine hundred Wampanoag. Included in his posthumous message was a plea to "stay away from organized religion, from the white man's religion."

There is validity in Chief Slow Turtle's wariness of church institutions and structures. The painful truth is that we often stray from Jesus' vision of God's reign—"on earth as in heaven." We frequently forget Micah's words to Israel about valuing outward form while forgetting to do what God has required. We overlook James's exhortation about pure and undefiled religion (James 1:27).

We neglect to practice the spiritual disciplines that Foster identifies as outward disciplines—those that minister to the needs of others in the world around us. Simplicity is a discipline related to our lifestyle choices; a simple lifestyle minimizes the clutter that so easily entangles and distracts. Similarly, solitude is a discipline of simplifying the environment, even if only temporarily, reducing your social circle to just God and yourself, the better to isolate the still, quiet voice in your spirit. Submission is a discipline that surrenders self to another, specifically to God—making yourself less so that God can be more—in your life and in the life of those around you. Service is the discipline that is most outward, perhaps, and it will often grow out of the others. It is making yourself available to God in order to meet the needs of others.

Most US Christians compartmentalize religion into particular times and places. Because churches today are incorporated, own property, seek zoning variances, receive tax-deductible contributions, and have officers and employees with personnel policies attached, it is easy to confuse the church with a business. But the church is the body of Christ, the continuing incarnation of Jesus on earth. We are members of this body. We are the arms and legs, the eyes and ears and the voices of Jesus as his living body. We assemble to renew our spirits for ministry in the world. We worship to come into the presence of the living God and hear afresh God's words and God's will.

I once met the minister of hospitality at a church in New York City. Their ushers pray for discernment to seat guests near those members who will make a connection. The prayer is an inward discipline and the goal is an outward act of service, of ministry to the least of these. Envision the potential transformation if your church were to become intentional about making everything it does a spiritual activity—no matter how routine or mundane the task may seem. That is a key to converting a church.

Support: The Corporate Disciplines

Finally, there is the call to "love kindness"—which one might deem consistent with John's exhortation that others will know we are Christian by our love for one another. Part of that love is cultivated through the practice of the corporate disciplines of worship, confession, guidance, and celebration. These are spiritual acts that occur in the community of faith—the means by which a church enters into corporate fellowship with God and with its individual members. In a very real sense, these are the disciplines that knit together the body of Christ and animate it with God's own lovingkindness.

Read the familiar story about the valley of dry bones in Ezekiel 37. God instructed Ezekiel to prophesy to the dry bones (Israel) and declare, "Hear the word of the Lord." The metaphor of parched bones scattered across the valley communicated the impossibility of new life for the congregation of Israel. Now read the passage again, substituting the word *churches* for *bones*. It is a sobering paraphrase. Congregations can be like these bones, coming together with noisy activity and having all the appearance of life (sinews and flesh) but lacking the breath that is life itself. But in this text is a word for dry churches that have lost hope and think new life is impossible. The breath (i.e., spirit) came from the four winds, and a vast multitude of the slain lived and stood on their feet. The concluding promise to Israel, and to all households of God, is that we are God's people, made alive because God's Spirit is within us. We may be assured that God still speaks, "Hear the word of the Lord," and when God speaks, God will also act to bring those words to pass (vv. 13-14).

An easy starting point toward becoming a converted church—one that possesses a renewed commitment to corporate worship and connection—is to seek radical change. That change is radical in the etymological sense of the word, meaning to go back to our roots in a pattern of giftedness and ministries as depicted in the New Testament (as described in Step 1) and to return to the three-fold call of Micah 6:8, "to do justice, to love kindness, and to walk humbly with your God."

Consider the existing groups within the church. If your congregation is typical, you will discover three primary categories: support (or fellowship) groups, study groups, and service groups. What if all groups—e.g., board of trustees, Sunday school class, senior ministry—were a three-legged stool where the legs were support, study, and service? Thus, in each group, no matter what its primary purpose, members would cultivate inward, outward, and corporate disciplines. Beyond their administrative and service tasks, the trustees would also intercede in prayer and model a simpler lifestyle; the Sunday school class would meet not only to study the Scriptures but also to fellowship in regular hymn sings and to work with Habitat for Humanity; and in addition to their monthly bus trips, the seniors would mentor teens in the youth group and gather for Bible study.

Perhaps the area that best exemplifies a balanced approach to ministry in a converted church is hospitality. Converted churches practice the spiritual gift of hospitality, which involves intentional spirituality (inward disciplines), gracious service (outward disciplines), and warm community (corporate disciplines). Henri Nouwen rightly reminds us that hospitality is more than tea parties but the ability to welcome the alien and alienated, to accept others just as they are without judgment, to generously allow them into our space.[3] Or as Micah might have put it, it demands that we remember to do justice in welcoming all equally, to show kindness and mercy in meeting needs both physical and spiritual, and to walk humbly in the awareness that we were once strangers and aliens ourselves until God embraced us as part of the body of Christ.

Reflection/Action

1. Read Ezekiel 47:1-12, what I call the "leaking plumbing chapter." Water flowing out from under the east door of the temple brings new life every place it flows. In what ways do you see faith leaking out of the church and bringing new life to the community?

2. Plan for making all groups in the church holistic by including study, support, and service in their gatherings. Study groups can do a service project, service boards can set aside time for education, and fellowship ministries can pray for and nurture one another.

3. What if you took prayer seriously? What if your church took prayer seriously? How can your congregation be accountable to one another to take prayer seriously?

4. What are the spiritual disciplines, and what would the practice of them look like in our congregation? Make plans to focus on several of these disciplines over the next year.

"So you want the church to grow, but you don't want to add any services, or tamper with the worship service, and you're not sure about new people, especially those with tattoos?"

STEP 6

Count the Cost of Transformation
Luke 14:25-33

> Christ has no body but yours, No hands, no feet
> on earth but yours, . . . Yours are the feet with
> which he walks to do good, Yours are the hands,
> with which he blesses all the world.
>
> —Teresa of Avila[1]

What You Need to Count

1. Count the cost in people.
2. Count the cost in resources.
3. Count the cost in suffering.

A search committee interviewed me for the senior pastorate in a church near the New Jersey coast. The committee members shared their desire for church growth, and I asked them if they had counted the cost. They didn't understand the question. I spent an entire afternoon helping them to count the costs involved in growing the congregation, and ultimately they acknowledged that they were not ready for that magnitude of change. My encounter with that search committee reminded me of Jesus' exchange with the rich young ruler. The cost of following Jesus was too great, and the young man went away grieving (Matthew 19:16-22).

Church growth means finding other people sitting in our pew, parking farther away from the sanctuary, and not knowing everyone's name. Church growth means less intimate involvement of the pastor and leaders in the lives of each member. Church growth means new board and committee members who may make different decisions. Church growth means discontinuing programs that do not meet needs and developing ministries that stretch the comfort level of the old members. Church growth means extending hospitality to strangers by doing things that make them feel at home rather than perpetuating the comfortable patterns of the past. All of these changes have a cost attached—costs related to the people involved, the resources required, and the emotional and psychological demands made.

Count the Cost in People

The early church struggled with the relational cost of transformation. The process at the Jerusalem Council (Galatians 2:1-10) sheds light on how they met this challenge. Paul and Barnabas had "no small dissension and debate" with the Judaizers who insisted that circumcision was necessary for salvation (Acts 15:2). This dispute was brought before a council in Jerusalem. The discernment process is notable. Respected leaders were looked to as arbiters. Everyone was allowed to have his or her say. Scripture was cited. The work of the Spirit in the hearts and lives of Gentiles was offered as evidence. The precedence of Simon Peter opening the gospel to the Gentiles is rehearsed from the brief history of the church. Compromise was found. And in the end, the teaching of Moses that had been read in the synagogues for generations past about circumcision was changed. The council sent two leaders with Paul and Barnabas to interpret this decision. There is much insight here for change management in churches of the twenty-first century that are not unlike the church of the first century.

COUNT THE COST OF TRANSFORMATION

Following a week of meetings with an evangelist and a lay witness team, our church moderator knocked on the parsonage door one evening. The evangelist had stretched our traditional church with a new emphasis on the Holy Spirit and new experiences in relational small groups. The moderator, whose family had been members for generations and who had attended weekly services since he was an infant, was distressed. What he had experienced made him so uncomfortable that he wasn't sure he could be part of a church like that. It is at these junctures that we as leaders often panic and decide the cost of transformation is too high. I chose to stand firm—and in my case, the risk paid off. The moderator did not leave the church and lived through many other changes, including the radical introduction of contemporary worship music and a praise band. He didn't like all of the changes, but he was so bonded to this congregation by his long history that he stayed to see the growth that followed.

Not everyone is bonded by history and extended family and will stay to see how the change develops. Some will stay—and resist. Are you prepared to count the cost of such rooted resistance? It may divide loyalties and undermine the authority of the leaders. It may disrupt ministry efforts and distract from the vision. It may damage the congregation's reputation and delay growth in the short run. Are you willing to pay the price and consider it an investment that will net greater returns in the future? Sometimes, the cost in congregational relationships is the most difficult to quantify. We have a tendency to underestimate it and the related costs that develop as a consequence, such as decreased tithes and increased stress. Those are the next costs a leader of congregational transformation must count.

Count the Cost in Resources
Naturally, the cost of renewal encompasses the pragmatic element of finances. Church growth inevitably places greater demands on leaders—and those demands may require the hiring

of additional pastors and increase in ministries and program staff. Significant growth in membership may force the issue of a capital campaign to build a larger sanctuary or an annex to the Christian education wing.

Jesus teaches about the cost of discipleship in Luke 14:25-33. He uses two vivid illustrations to explain discipleship. He asks the people in the crowd if they would build a tower without first estimating the cost and knowing they had enough money to complete the project. The alternative is public ridicule when the foundation is laid and the walls are unfinished. He asks the crowd again to consider whether a king would go to war without considering whether his ten thousand soldiers can defeat an army of twenty thousand. If not, that king sends a delegation to negotiate terms of peace.

This pragmatic Jesus flies in the face of our usual understanding of his message. Is this the same Jesus who told the disciples "nothing will be impossible for you" if they had faith as small as a seed of mustard (Matthew 17:20-21)? Now he is teaching that we should have enough money in the bank for our renewal strategy and know where the leaders will come from before we start. Where is the faith in only building towers when the building fund has reached its goal or in going into battle with at least even, if not superior, odds? The answer to this seeming contradiction is to look at the context: the cost of discipleship.

There are also human resources, whether volunteer or paid, to consider. Some years ago, I heard an Indian missionary tell the story of pastors from the villages in his state meeting for prayer and pleading with God to send a revival. Their fervent prayers were answered. Whole villages were converted. But they had not counted the cost. The cost was neither loss of members nor insufficient finances. The cost was in human resources—a lack of leaders who were trained and equipped to minister to the thousands of converts who lined up to be instructed and baptized. The pastors whose prayers had been answered were exhausted. If they had only known that their prayers would unleash such a powerful movement of the Spirit, they might have been better prepared! They might have initiated leadership training in advance, in expectation of the explosion to come.

The story raises awkward issues for those praying for renewal. Do we really expect God to hear and respond to our prayers? Do we have faith enough to prepare now for answered prayers in the future? Will we be able to change to provide leaders for the new church God is creating? The issue suggests the story of the invalid that Jesus healed at the pool of Bethesda, of whom Jesus first asked, "Do you want to be made well?" (John 5:6). Do our churches want to be made well?

Ask any church member if he or she would like the church to be well, to stand up and walk, to grow and be healthy, and the answer is invariably yes. Paradoxically, however, members are often resistant to the changes and commitment needed for health, growth, transformation, and renewal. There can be no cheap transformation.

Count the Cost in Suffering

Tony Campolo tells a story about Søren Kierkegaard. Kierkegaard witnessed a Danish pastor, dressed in his satin and velvet robes, reading from a gilded Bible on a mahogany lectern with silk paraments, "If any want to become my followers, let them deny themselves and take up their cross and follow me." Kierkegaard reportedly said, "And no one even laughed." This pale imitation of discipleship offended Kierkegaard. He saw no suffering cross or self-denial evident in the state church in Denmark and brutally satirized this distortion of the gospel. Authentic discipleship that transforms persons, churches, and communities costs something.

In the parable in Luke 14, Jesus was sifting the large crowd who would join his movement by using common-sense examples of construction and warfare to caution them against being joiners. The cost of following Jesus is to "hate father and mother, wife and children, brothers and sisters, yes, and even life itself" to "carry the cross and follow" him (Luke 14:26-27). In the same way that the building contractor and the military general count the cost, so those who would follow Jesus must anticipate that this is a huge commitment. Church transformation is also a huge commitment. Every transformation initiative we have undertaken nationally and regionally had, and will have, dropouts. Those who underestimate the size of the commitment required to bring authentic renewal to Christ's church often experience sticker shock or buyer's remorse later, and they opt out. Those who mistake the opportunity for deep organizational change for another program or emphasis will be disappointed when what appears to be renewal evaporates and the status quo returns.

The fallibility of the first disciples always comforts me at this point. Jesus' job description to be one of his followers demands everything, and Jesus takes on a group who apparently did not count on Calvary. Jesus will likewise teach and coach us through Scripture and stretch us when our plans are different from his plans. Jesus did not replace any of his fallible first followers. He worked with this unlikely group he believed could be the foundation of Christendom and gave them the leadership gifts, experiences, and Holy Spirit they would need to continue his work.

Reflection/Action

1. Jesus taught that discipleship is costly. When has discipleship been costly for you or your congregation?

2. Five Whys is a simple exercise that can yield profound insights. Choose a proposition such as "Our church has not reached its full potential or moved toward its preferred future" or

"Our church is hesitant to change." List five reasons why for your proposition. Now, for each of the five reasons, look more closely and find five reasons for each of the five reasons. If any of these seems like an especially fruitful area to pursue, it is possible to go another round. What would be the cost of removing some of these blocks to transformation?

3. Imagine what your church would be like and what behaviors you would observe in members and leaders after a metamorphosis. A cocoon and butterfly would be the right visual image. Responses to this question can be written on a butterfly cutout or image. On the reverse side, estimate the personal and congregational cost of each change.

Finally, a church that doesn't suffer from
the "Lone Ranger Syndrome."

STEP 7

Unmask Your Lone Rangers
Ephesians 4:11-16

God governs in the affairs of man. And if a sparrow cannot fall to the ground without his notice, is it probable that an empire can rise without His aid? We have been assured in the Sacred Writings that except the Lord build the house, they labor in vain that build it. I firmly believe this. I also believe that, without His concurring aid, we shall succeed in this political building no better than the builders of Babel.

—Benjamin Franklin,
Constitutional Convention of 1787

What You Need to Expose
1. Expose insular and self-sufficient tendencies.
2. Expose elitist attitudes toward the laity.
3. Expose the spiritual gifts of the congregation.

"Who was that masked man?" The 1933 radio series gave us the legend of a Texas Ranger who was the lone survivor of an ambush by the Cavendish gang. This masked cowboy galloped about the Old West righting injustices. The Lone Ranger has become a cliché for those who try to do it alone. Don't attempt church renewal alone. After all, even the Lone Ranger had his clever and laconic friend

Tonto, the faithful steed Silver, his nephew Dan Reid, and the retired ranger who worked his silver mine. The Lone Ranger leader cannot accomplish enduring church change and congregational transformation. It is essential that the transformation process be a team effort.

Masks of a Lone Ranger Leader

Doc Do-It-Myself. This Lone Ranger leader lives by the mantra, "If you want it done right, do it yourself." To be fair, many times it *is* quicker and easier to produce an excellent result by yourself rather than to take the time to teach and coach someone else to produce the same result. Others won't do it as well at first, and they may never do it exactly the same way, but this attitude and practice not only limits the growth of others but also limits what you are able to accomplish in the long run. Regrettably, a recovering do-it-myself leader will often morph into a microminister, given to micromanaging every detail that she or he cautiously or reluctantly delegates. The tendency continues to reflect a need for control and an insistence on having everything develop according to the leader's plan and preferences.

Rev. to the Rescue! Picture an R on a Superman cape. Some Lone Ranger leaders have strong emotional needs to be the hero or heroine and single-handedly raise a sinking ship. Often, this kind of leader plays into the unhealthy expectations of the congregation, creating or continuing a codependent pastor-congregation relationship. Not only does this create a passive and stunted congregation, but also it leads to burnout in the leader. Rescuers inevitably find themselves in need of rescue, but they are unable or unwilling to ask for help. In part, they fear exposing their own vulnerability, perceiving that a request for help is a sign of weakness. They may also fear rejection or ridicule. What's worse, because the Rescue Rev. has always done it all for his or her followers, the congregation is likely to be ill-equipped to provide help if asked.

Committee Commander. A group of people at a meeting or doing a task together is not a team. Some Lone Rangers create the illusion of team building or delegating by forming a plethora of committees and boards, but in reality, these groups function only to carry out the instructions or vision of the leader. They have no real autonomy in vision casting or decision making, and they are often arbitrarily convened. In contrast, teams are organic and dynamic. They capitalize on individual gifts, covering one member's weakness with another's strength. They know each other's spiritual journey and life history, pray for and encourage one another, and learn and serve together.

Pastor-in-Chief. This Lone Ranger leader takes Committee Commander to the next level of authoritarian function. Laity are perceived as second-class citizens of the kingdom, essential but only for the purpose of taking orders and executing the general's commands. This tendency toward authoritarian leadership is contrary to the life of the church described in the New Testament (see 1 Corinthians 12:12-26). This tendency often produces meteoric leaders—pastors who streak through the life of the church in a blaze of glory only to be burned up in the atmosphere of everyday life. The Pastor-in-Chief also fails to mentor and disciple people in their faith journey and spiritual gifts—and the usual result is a church that flickers out once its shooting-star general has been extinguished.

We consistently observe that Lone Ranger leaders are neutralized and derailed. So why do church leaders continue to try to do the work of ministry and transformation by themselves? I think there are three critical insights to expose if we are to succeed in unmasking the Lone Rangers in the Christian church today.

Insular and Self-Sufficient Tendencies

In nearly every instance, renewal breaks in from outside the circle or center of professional clergy. Nagaland, a state in northeast India, is a good example. Radical transformation began with a children's group that met at the church after school and waited on the Lord in prayer and confession, often late into the night. Renewal began among the least literate members of congregations and was evidenced by a change of behavior, a changed lifestyle, and loyalty to the Word of God. Next the Spirit touched high school students and brought about a fresh perspective for mission and evangelism. The church then began sending missionaries to nearby villages. Prayer meetings were convened every Monday in government offices and every Tuesday in schools. Outreach meetings with butchers and taxi drivers were typical of the creative evangelism. The message penetrated every corner of the community, and faith in Christ brought honesty and integrity to daily life and work. Nagaland is now 90 percent Christian in what is an overwhelmingly Hindu nation.

There are countless examples of renewal breaking in from the outside rather than being manufactured by the leaders, especially a lone leader, on the inside. The First Baptist Church in America experienced renewal when a prison church began worshipping in their meeting-house. A street hockey team of neighborhood teens refreshed an aging church in suburban Philadelphia. Revival among the gypsies in Spain has brought new vitality to the Protestant church in that country.

Lone Rangers must be unmasked if real transformation is to occur. A mask obscures our ability to see clearly where the Spirit of God is moving and what the power of Jesus is working in the community around our insular and self-*in*sufficient world.

Elitist Attitudes and Assumptions

I met with pastors in North Jersey to stretch their understanding of the ministry of the whole people of God. I wanted them to understand that the vitality of their churches did not depend solely on them. Most struggled with the idea that laity were ministers in spite of reasoned explanations about the meaning of laity and minister and the absence of clergy in Scripture. *Kleros*, a Greek word meaning "lot," "that which is assigned by lot," "allotment," or metaphorically, "heritage," is the closest we get to our English word *clergy* in the Bible. There are too many professional clergy paid to do the work of ministry who are not at all concerned about empowerment of others (see Easum's grid in Step 3) who could join in the expansion of ministry. Just as "mission is what we pay others to do" rather than what we do, is a distortion of the New Testament, so the lone ranger clergy is a distortion of the biblical pattern.

"The Comma Heresy" has been my exaggerated description of the theological error caused by a punctuation mistake in Ephesians 4:12. Paul instructs the Ephesians (vv. 11-12) that Christ who gave the gift of grace also gave gifts that "some [should be] apostles; some, prophets; and some, evangelists; and some, pastors and teachers; for the perfecting of the saints, for the work of the ministry, for the edifying of the body of Christ" (KJV). There is no punctuation in the earliest Greek manuscripts, and punctuation represents a translator's interpretation. The translators of the King James Version (1611) projected onto the text their own cultural realities where professional clergy were doing the work of ministry. That understanding is turned upside down by the removal of a key comma, resulting in translations that read "to equip the saints for the work of ministry" (NRSV) and "to prepare God's people for works of service" (NIV). I like Eugene Peterson's paraphrase in *The Message*, "to train Christians in skilled servant work." Ministry is not the solitary responsibility of the ordained but the joint effort of the whole people of God.

Spiritual Gifts in the Body

Another misunderstanding of the church, rooted in centuries of understanding the church as an institution, is to consider apostles, prophets, evangelists, and pastor-teachers as people who have offices instead of gifts. These are not only the vocations of people we call to be full-time missionaries, preachers, pastors, or Christian educators. These are among the gifts the Holy Spirit has given to every baptized believer. The church is full of underemployed ministers who are shepherds, disciple makers, communicators, and teachers. Paul reminds the Corinthians that the church is the body of Christ, his continuing presence on earth after the Ascension, and that the body does not consist of one member but of many. There are many members but only one body. All of the members are indispensable (1 Corinthians 12:12-31). This organic understanding of members is preferred over the organizational understanding revealed in membership rosters and reports. Peter writes to the Christian diaspora that they should be "good stewards of the manifold grace of God" and "serve one another with whatever gift each of you has received" (1 Peter 4:10). Clearly the New Testament church did not imagine Lone Rangers. Clearly ministry is a team enterprise.

What were the talents that the servants invested and buried in Jesus' parable of the talents (Matthew 25:14-30)? They would not be natural abilities. That would be reading our modern usage back into the text. A first-century talent was a unit of weight measurement or a monetary unit. It was worth more than fifteen years' wages of a laborer. What valuable gift has God given us to invest in the kingdom of heaven?

If Jesus called the Twelve and appointed seventy, if the disciples chose seven deacons, and if Paul always had missionary companions, why are church leaders so resistant to shared leadership and team ministry and so prone to try to fix the church by themselves?

A vision community, a true team of early adopters and influencers, is a useful strategy to disarm those who see this as the leader's responsibility. One of the joys of my last pastorate is to look back and see those I encouraged in leadership thriving and the initiatives we planted continuing. One of the most painful things to hear was that some of the pastor's groupies left the church after I left the church. That suggests that the lone relationship was with the pastor and those individuals had not been assimilated into membership or shared in any of the ministry. I recognize that this is a danger, although I understand that transference of pastoral allegiance to congregational allegiance is a process for those whose initial encounters with the church are through pastoral care and life crises. Fortunately the perceived groupies were an exception. In our postmodern world it is less the case that the primary leader is the reason people stay at a church. Visitors look for congruence between the leader's words and the congregation's behavior. The more powerful attractor to Jesus is not his preachers but his people. The witness of faith and love authentically and transparently lived out by the community is contagious and is the opposite of superstar preachers and Lone Ranger pastors. The leader who doesn't mentor, equip laity for the work of ministry, train interns, take the long-range view, and perform as a team player and player-coach is doomed to be a shooting star at best.

Not doing it alone also applies to not doing it without God. Jesus calls disciples. The Lord God summons prophets. The Holy Spirit gifts leaders. We cannot forget the divine source of our call, our ministry, and our strength.

Reflection/Action

1. Ephesians 4:16 echoes Psalm 139:13-15. The psalmist writes, "For it was you who formed my inward parts; you knit me together in my mother's womb. I praise you that I am fearfully and wonderfully made." God fearfully and wonderfully makes every church. Reflect on the interdependence of Christ's body, the continuing incarnation.

2. "Baptism is our ordination to ministry" is a declaration about the ministry of the whole people of God. What are your biblical understandings of ordination and commissioning for ministry? Of roles and understandings of laity (literally, "people") and clergy (literally, "what is assigned by lot")?

3. "Zapp! Empowerment for Ministry" was a conference focusing on the ministry of the laity. A leader of our denominational men's ministry challenged my use of "empowerment." Only God empowers! Yet, many church leaders disempower church members. What are the reasons you tend to be a solo leader, and what blocks are there to truly equipping the saints for the work of ministry?

4. What is something you have been doing as a lone ranger? How might you empower others to help with this? What are the concrete steps?

STEP 8

Persist in the Process
Luke 10:1-20

The essential thing "in heaven and earth" is . . .
that there should be long obedience in the same
direction; there thereby results, and has always
resulted in the long run, something which has
made life worth living.
    —Friedrich Nietzsche, *Beyond Good and Evil*[1]

What You Need to Grasp
1. Renewal is a process.
2. Process demands cooperation.
3. Cooperation takes time.

"I am tired of the sound of helicopters; I want to hear the sound of jazz." This was the lament of Mayor C. Ray Nagin of New Orleans following the devastation of Hurricane Katrina. He was in a hurry to repopulate the city and reopen the Cajun restaurants and jazz clubs and unique culture of New Orleans, but the levees were only temporarily repaired and the Ninth Ward would flood again when the next hurricane brushed by. Nagin was severely criticized for encouraging people to return without water, sewers, electricity, telephone service, 911 emergency services, or a plan for rebuilding New Orleans.

Church leaders also grow tired of the sound of helicopters. The rotors remind us that there is an emergency, rescuers are needed, extraordinary effort is needed to repair the breach in the levees, interventions are called for, and normal life is interrupted. "Jazz" for the church leader is the wistful desire for everything to be alive and vibrant again.

Renewal Is a Process

When my son was a preteen, he collected Transformers. These toys looked like ordinary trucks but could be manipulated into robots. Transformation? Not really. Pieces of plastic had been rearranged and appeared to be something else, but the essential makeup of the toy was unchanged. This is often how the church approaches renewal. We rearrange the parts so that it appears different, but nothing substantive changes.

The challenge is there is no just-add-water or pop-in-the-microwave church transformation or leader transformation. It is a process. There are no books, seminars, strategies, consultants, or events that guarantee revival. There are no shortcuts—unless God chooses to act through the miraculous intervention of the Holy Spirit.

Consider the testimony of Scripture. Some things are instant in the Bible: the conversion of Saul on the road to Damascus and the water changed into wine at a wedding in Cana, for example. However, the lasting transformation of people—of fishermen and tax collectors and sinners—into faithful disciples of Jesus, that was a process. It is helpful to remember that the Greek word translated "disciple" in the Bible is the word for student or apprentice. Jesus spent three years with the Twelve, teaching and coaching them, and their discipleship grades are not always exemplary. Just reading Matthew's Gospel we find: "Why are you afraid, you of little faith?" (8:26); "You of little faith, why did you doubt?" (14:31); "You of little faith, why are you talking about having no bread?" (16:8); "Get behind me, Satan! You are a stumbling block to me; for you are setting your mind not on divine things but human things" (16:23); "Truly I tell you, one of you will betray me" (26:21); and "You will all become deserters because of me this night" (26:31). It is only in the Acts of the Apostles, after the resurrection and gifting of the Holy Spirit, that we see mature and confident apostles. There was a significant learning curve—a process—involved in becoming a disciple of Christ.

There is a similar process inherent in church renewal. Just consider: Discipleship is about the personal transformation of a single individual, and church renewal is about the transformation of an entire congregation of such individuals, all of whom are at varying stages in the discipleship process.

Process Demands Cooperation

That brings us to our second important point. Because church renewal is a process, it requires a spirit of cooperation. It demands that spiritual formation on a personal level be extended and networked at the congregational level. Remember the illustration of the Transformer toy? It is not enough merely to rearrange your human resources, form new committees, and shuffle your programs. True transformation requires essential and substantive change—of individual members and then of the congregation.

To start a discussion about church change, I often use an activity involving a set of Tinkertoys. I divide the Tinkertoys into piles with different pieces and quantities in each pile. I assign each pile to a group of four or five persons and instruct each group to build a church without any spoken conversation between group members. The church can be a literal representation of a steepled building or a symbolic representation of the people and mission. Typically a vision and leader emerges, a church changer and resistance to change appear, followers and helpers contribute, and occasionally an individual or two remain on the periphery, either excluded and ignored or simply content to observe.

The challenge in the activity is that some of the groups are missing critical or sufficient pieces; perhaps they have all connector rods but no spools or joints to connect them. Other groups have an abundance of pieces with some left over. What I find fascinating is that never in my years of using this activity has it ever occurred to a group that they might combine efforts and resources with other groups—or that they might help another group by giving or exchanging spools and rods. Why doesn't it occur to anyone to cooperate with a neighboring group? After all, they have all been given the same task, and they all have the same basic resources at their disposal to accomplish the job. (The parallels in the task of building the Christian church are obvious.)

So the question becomes how to lead a church in the change process, particularly when the process demands cooperation among a diverse group of individuals. One helpful concept is *diffusion of innovation*. Formulated in 1903, diffusion of innovation theory—understanding the way new ideas are adopted—has become a hot topic with the publication of a book by Everett Rogers.[2] Rogers reported on a study conducted by two sociologists, Bryce Ryan and Neil Gross, dealing with the diffusion of hybrid corn seed among Iowa farmers. Ryan and Gross classified the segments of Iowa farmers in relation to the amount of time it took them to adopt an innovation—in this case, the hybrid corn seed. The five segments (or categories) of farmers who adopted the hybrid corn seed were innovators (2.5%), early adopters (13.5%), early majority (34%), late majority (34%), and laggards (16%).

Rogers showed that all innovations spread through society in an S-curve, as innovators select a new idea first and are followed by the early adopters, the early majority, and the late majority, until an idea is commonly embraced. Consider how awareness of this principle in leading church change can save a leader much frustration. Apply the insights by looking for the innovators and early adopters in your congregation. Cast your vision for renewal first to them, and then to the early majority. Obtain their cooperation, not only in implementing the change but also in courting the cooperation and buy-in of others. Be patient with the late majority and laggards. After all, renewal is a process—and they are a part of the process.

Cooperation Takes Time

Discernment of a vision for renewal takes time. Congregational spiritual formation takes time. Establishment of new values and priorities takes time. Developing new ways of organizing and serving takes time. Then to have those changes become broadly owned and thoroughly lived out—that cooperative facet of the transformation process is especially time consuming.

Consider an example from an individual life. A woman who had for years been a Christmas-Easter church attender had a profound conversion experience. Was it an instant change? For the woman, it may have seemed like Paul's experience on the Damascus Road. However, her mother-in-law confided in me that she had been praying for that woman for twenty-five years. For the person who had been desperately seeking transformation in that woman's life, the conversion was merely the culmination of a long and prayerfully inspired process of inward renewal. In congregations as well as in individual people, there may be a tipping point from which noticeable change can be seen. It is likely that prayer and preparation preceded the tipping point.

My files are filled with stories of churches that did not understand the process of renewal. Discipleship, like the seed that is planted and grows into grain, is something that takes time.

I helped birth a renewal strategy based on the text in 2 Timothy 1:6. It was intended that churches would covenant to participate for three to four years. According to church renewal experts, it takes this long or longer to change the culture of an organization. There were many joiners who were anxious for the "jazz" of renewal to begin but not many committed to persist in the process over the years.

Discouraged with the pace of the process and the lack of congregational cooperation with change, pastors left their churches. Churches that mistakenly understood renewal as a program moved on to other programs when they tired of the process. A pastor in New Jersey who led his congregation through an intentional journey of renewal with initially good results later met significant opposition and lost church families dissatisfied with changes. He described the discouragement of the congregation as "renewal fatigue."

No Instant Renewal

At the beginning of the new millennium, Ed Silvosa spoke at a national evangelism conference. He is well known for his emphasis on prayer and community evangelism strategies. His exegesis of Luke 10:1-12, the sending of the seventy, forever changed the way I understand and describe evangelism as well as reinforced my belief that there is no instant evangelism, no instant discipleship, and no instant church renewal.

Silvosa reframes the way the church has traditionally thought about evangelism: invite people to believe in Jesus, invite them to join the church fellowship, and finally experience the blessings of God. Silvosa flips this understanding upside down when he points to the pattern in Luke 10. Jesus' first instruction to the pairs of disciples he sends into the towns is to say, "Peace to this house" (v. 5). The first act of evangelism is to offer a blessing. The next instruction is to "remain in the same house, eating and drinking whatever they provide . . . eat what is set before you" (vv. 7-8). The second act of evangelism is table fellowship with unbelievers. Third, the thirty-five teams are to respond to human need: "cure the sick" (v. 9). Last, the seventy are to announce, "The kingdom of God has come near to you" (v. 9). After blessing, after fellowship, after meeting needs, the gospel is preached.

This pattern of evangelism requires us to extend ourselves toward others and be involved in their lives and needs. This approach demands that we live an evangelistic lifestyle in which our character and consistency is part of our witness. The New Testament does not tell us how many towns were visited by the seventy, how many towns received them and how many rejected them, or how many months elapsed between verses 10 and 17, when the "seventy returned with joy." But we can be sure this relational evangelism took considerable time.

This passage is instructive not only for the processes of evangelism and discipleship but also for principles for church transformers. This list of don'ts refers to congregational transformation.

1. Don't do it alone. Jesus sent them out in pairs. Support and accountability are essential in ministry.

2. Don't do it without a plan or itinerary. Jesus decided which towns and places they should visit. It is better if the plan has a biblical basis.

3. Don't be discouraged by the labor shortage. Two people sent with a plan from Jesus were adequate to reach an entire town with the Good News of the kingdom of God.

4. Don't think it depends on material resources. Jesus asked them to have faith that their needs will be provided, "for the laborer deserves to be paid" (Luke 10:7).

5. Don't think that it depends on human ingenuity. The seventy reported to Jesus, "Lord, in your name even the demons submit to us!" (v. 17).

6. Don't expect that your personal preferences will be more important than the mission. The ancient dictum about unity in essentials and charity in nonessentials is still true. Twice Jesus reminded them to eat what was set before them. Even kosher preferences were secondary to building Christ's church.

7. Don't expect to succeed all the time. Jesus told the seventy that there would be towns where they are not welcome and houses where their "shalom" will be rebuffed.

8. Don't take credit for the victories. Jesus cautioned the seventy not to rejoice because of the power and authority, which he had given them, but to rejoice that their names were written in heaven (vv. 19-20).

Old-Time Religion or Old-Fashioned Revival

"Old-fashioned" in a church context conjures images of old-time tent revivals: sawdust floors, emotional singing, and protracted altar calls while a Hammond organ coaxed more verses of "Just As I Am" out of the crowd. This is not what I mean when I say old-fashioned. By old-fashioned I mean the Ante-Nicene, pre-Constantinian church before gifts had reified into offices. By old-fashioned I mean waiting on the Lord rather than taking matters into our own hands. By old-fashioned I mean returning to biblical principles that preceded church bylaws, Robert's Rules of Order, and corporate America as the model for the church.

Revivals are mostly synonymous with what we now call preaching missions. We have updated the form with festival venues, contemporary music, contextual music (e.g., hip-hop), celebrity testimonies, drama, and media. But the focus is still on a moment for participants to decide to follow Jesus. The root meaning of revival is "to live again." The modifier *old-fashioned* points backward, back beyond revivalism as it was practiced in the United States, back to ancient and biblical principles and methods to breathe life anew (*anakaino*) into the body of Christ. It points back to a time when everyone in a city belonged to the one church and membership had nothing to do with buildings and everything to do with the body of Christ and its interdependent parts.

Reflection/Action

1. In the ministry of the seventy you might imagine instant (or revolutionary) change for those who embraced their message and

gradual (or incremental) change for the disciples as they learned by doing. When have you experienced change in each of these ways?

2. Remembering the theory about diffusion of innovation, are you an innovator, an early adopter in the early or late majority, or a laggard? What is the mix of these types in your congregation? How will you bring along the late adopters and laggards?

3. Create a survey about your church and interview persons in your neighborhood, in a nearby park, or at the mall. Use open-ended questions about the purpose of the church and general impressions about Christians, your denomination, and local churches, including your own. Report survey results to leaders and the congregation asking about the implications.

4. What traditions have grown threadbare in your congregation? How might you update those traditions so that they are contemporary, relevant, and honoring of the heritage they originally represented? For example, crusade evangelism, where persons gather in a stadium, is replaced with festival evangelism in open spaces with music and drama and other attractions that precede the evangelistic preaching.

In the ocean of life, Horace
underestimated the ripples of change.

STEP 9

Make the Connections
1 Corinthians 12:12-26

We are caught in an inescapable network of mutu-
ality, tied in a single garment of destiny.
> —Martin Luther King Jr.,
> "Letter from a Birmingham Jail"

What You Need to Connect
1. Connect with the culture.
2. Connect with the context.
3. Connect with the congregation.
4. Connect with scriptural precedents.

At their one-hundred-fiftieth anniversary celebration, I asked the congregation of the Aldenville Baptist Church in northeastern
Pennsylvania what a local revival service, hemlock trees, the Irish
potato famine, a New York City church, and an upstate New York
leather baron had to do with the founding of their church. All of these
disparate factors had converged in 1855 and influenced the founding
of their church. Hemlock trees have bark that is rich in tannin, the
substance needed in the leather tanning process. A family named
Alden were tanners by trade, so a financier from New York, who was
already invested in shoe leather, bankrolled the family to build a tan-
nery near a large stand of hemlock trees. A population center (later

named Aldenville for its first family) grew up around the factory, largely formed by single immigrant workers who had fled the potato famine in Ireland. About the same time, Elder Henry Curtis, a pastor and church planter from the oldest Baptist church in New York City, was preaching nearby. Curtis invited another pastor to preach a revival in the Aldenville neighborhood, and many people made commitments of faith and were baptized. This provided the critical mass to petition the local Baptist Association to form a new church.

Everything is indeed connected, sometimes in ways that are unseen. Other times, everything is connected in ways that are all too obvious, as in the blue-collar congregation in an old steel mill town where the declining population and depressed economy of the community were reflected in the congregation. Community issues of low self-esteem and domestic violence came to church on Sunday. For better or worse, everything is connected. When approaching the task of church renewal, it is vital that a leader recognize existing connections and make additional connects.

Connect with the Culture

Culture wars play themselves out in the church. Denominations and congregations are frequently polarized like politically red and blue states. Homosexuality, abortion, the role of women, creationism, divorce, war, poverty, public education, the environment, religion in the public square, and immigration are a few of the visceral issues that divide. In *Our Endangered Values: America's Moral Crisis,* former president Jimmy Carter recalls the newly elected president of the Southern Baptist Convention coming to visit him in the Oval Office. As the man and his wife were leaving, the religious leader said, "We are praying, Mr. President, that you will abandon secular humanism as your religion."[1] Carter's appointment of women to high positions of government, among many other issues, had put Carter at odds with conservatives. Churches are forced to make choices that align them with the culture or against the culture, but they always exist within the culture. What is in the newspaper and on CNN comes to church also.

The church is located in a "post" world—postdenominational, postmodern, postliterate, and post-Christian world. We ignore the impact of those realities on the local church at our peril. Brand-name loyalty has been disappearing in the larger culture and can be seen by members switching between churches, the low awareness of denominational identity, the naming and renaming of churches, pastors who come from nondenominational seminaries, and shrinking membership even among denominations that are not mainline.

In the modern era, traced to the Age of Enlightenment, the church and clergy were highly respected institutions and professions, truth and morality were absolute, apologetics and theology were rational, and mission was over there. In contrast, the latest edition of the National Council of Churches's *Yearbook of American and Canadian Churches* is subtitled *Postmodern Christianity: Emergent Church and Blogs*.[2] Internet technologies such as blogs and podcasts are words that my spell-checker doesn't know yet,[3] but they join XBox video games and DVDs as ways that people seek spirituality. Pastor, author, and emergent church leader Brian McLaren describes denominational distinctives as "marginal notes" in his eclectic spirituality that borrows from Eastern Orthodoxy and Pentecostalism and everything in between. That is the essence of the postmodern emergent church.[4]

Church consultant Loren Mead has famously remarked that God is dismantling denominations as fast as God can and noted that with the end of Christendom we live in an age like the *apost*olic period (notice the word *post* here also), when society was indifferent or unfriendly to Christians. In the United States, there are more Muslims than Episcopalians, Salvation Army bell ringers are unwelcome at big box stores, communities oppose the expansion of church properties with the same zeal that was once reserved for liquor outlets or X-rated bookstores, and employees are asked not to wear Christian symbols. This post-Christian challenge need not be a threat but like all realities can be an opportunity to do mission at your doorstep by paying attention to your culture, just as the first-century church did.

Connect with the Context

What happens in our lives from the past and present is alive in the church. If we grow up in a family that does not express affection with hugs or if touch is abusive, we will be uncomfortable with the hugging and intimacy expressed in some congregations. All of the issues of church conflict connect to our experiences of conflict in our families of origin and other settings (see Step 4 again). Codependents are especially prone to enabling unhealthy behavior and allowing the desire for harmony to trump the need to confront conflict. As in Charles Dickens's *A Christmas Carol*, all of our ghosts come to church with us. It is naïve to think that we can compartmentalize our family, community, workplace, and church experiences. Our personal histories, our individual context, are inextricably connected to who and how we are in the church and the world today.

What happens within the church is connected to everything, just as the gears and parts of an old-fashioned grandfather clock are connected to the hour and minute hands. We may only see the clock face and present time or perhaps the weights and pendulum, but inside the cabinet is another world. And behind that physical world is the history of the clock, perhaps a family heirloom that conjures stories of ancestors past, a clockmaker, and a tale of technology. Outside the clock are the events and lives scheduled by time—all connected. The church is a similarly complex, interconnected system. When we attempt change, we are not working with only one part of a system. The smallest change changes the entire system. That is why the resonance of a leader who is spiritually and relationally healthy reverberates positively throughout the entire congregation. That is also why the dissonance of a burned-out or rusted-out leader reverberates negatively throughout the entire congregation.

Connect with the Congregation

Another layer of diverse and complex connections is the presence of what Leadership Network describes as traditionalists, conservatives, progressives, and radicals in every church, just as in society.

Traditionalists argue for no change. Once change occurs, it becomes the new status quo. This group can react very emotionally to change and needs time to process change. This dynamic is easily seen in church hymnody. The innovative and resisted new music of each generation becomes the new status quo, and we quickly forget that the traditional, comfortable, and familiar music we prefer was also once controversial.

Conservatives value and can identify the benefits of the status quo. They will ask questions that need to be answered. They also will carry the financial weight if they buy into proposed changes. I designed a church planning retreat that produced some practical recommendations. The recommendations were researched, discussed at several meetings, and seemed to die in committee. It wasn't until a conservative took the lead and agreed to finance one of the proposals that the status quo changed.

Progressives anticipate growth needs, live on the growing edge, and will take calculated risks. Review plans with this group and use them as interpreters to conservatives. It was a group like this at First Baptist Church of Rio de Janeiro that began their mugging ministry. They saw the hordes of revelers around their church building at Carnivale and decide to reach out to petty criminals in the crowd. Church members banded tracts together and placed them conspicuously in their vest pockets. When a disappointed pickpocket discovered gospel tracts instead of a wallet full of money, there were a surprising number of opportunities for gospel conversations.

Radicals are the source of ideas. They create, stir up, and excite life in the church. However, they are also a group that tends to burn out quickly. They are rarely a source of leadership, not only because they lack stamina and discipline but also because they are typically unable or unwilling to bring others alongside. For related reasons, they are also not a good group to screen new ideas with because their endorsement is rarely compelling to the majority.

As a leader, you need to have an accurate understanding of which members of your congregation fall into which sociopolitical group, and you need to know how those groups connect to one another as well as to the issues on the table. If they do not connect, it is incumbent on the leader to facilitate making those connections. Radicals might generate new ideas, but those ideas should be screened through and endorsed by your progressives, who are better equipped to translate those ideas in more palatable terms to the conservatives in the congregation. In turn, the conservatives may be positioned to court cautious support or patient tolerance from the traditionalists. And having a good feel for how each group is positioned in relation to personal or congregational history as well as to contemporary culture is another vital connection to make.

Connect with Scriptural Precedents

By scanning the culture, the historical and personal contexts, and the congregation for connections, the church leader becomes aware of the "body life" (*soma*) of a particular and local community of faith. The apostle Paul knew this all too well when he planted and nurtured a church at Corinth. He knew the difficulties of proclaiming Christ crucified, "a stumbling block to Jews and foolishness to Gentiles" (1 Corinthians 1:23). Jesus as Messiah was a tough sell in this cosmopolitan city. Paul would later hear of factions, quarrels, childishness, sexual immorality, lawsuits among believers, drunkenness at the Lord's Supper, denial of the resurrection, disorderly worship, and false apostles.

It is impossible to deconstruct fully the ways in which personal lives, secular culture and values, the religion of pagan temples and Jewish synagogue, and class and race intertwined within this early church. But what Scripture does describe offers valuable material for the leader to pay attention to. The unhealthy way in which the parts were connected was a spiritual problem and prompted Paul's familiar words in 1 Corinthians 12. In verses 12-26 Paul teaches the Corinthians that the church is one body with many members. Weak and strong. Honorable and respectable and less so. All connected and interdependent. "If one member suffers, all suffer together with it; if one member is honored, all rejoice together with it" (1 Corinthians 12:26).

At an adult retreat, we recruited four volunteers. Three of them we blindfolded: to the first we gave a pitcher of water; to the second we gave a cup; the third was supposed to be given a drink from the first two. The fourth person served as the eyes and gave instructions to the hands pouring and offering the drink. It was a little messy, but the activity illustrated how we depend on each other to do the work of Christ's church.

What does a healthy, balanced body life look like in a local church?[5] In my own denomination, we perceive the means and end of congregational renewal and transformation to be the disciple-making church. Therefore, we use a holistic assessment model called the "Qualities of a "Disciple-Making Church."[6] It is an excellent checklist of interdependent qualities essential for congregational vitality and indicator of areas for formation and transformation. The disciple-making congregation charts its course by the words of Jesus in John 15:1-2, 5: "I am the true vine, and my Father is the vine grower. He removes every branch in me that bears no fruit. Every branch that bears fruit he prunes to make it bear more fruit . . . you are the branches. Those who abide in me and I in them bear much fruit; because apart from me you can do nothing."

Church transformation calls for encouragement and support in what is sometimes a demanding process. The result—healthy Christians continually deepening their relationships with God and others, equipped for service, ministering where called, and producing new believers—is worth the effort. These Christians make up a healthy, reproducing church. Renewed, disciple-making congregations live out the following qualities:

1. Spiritual and relational vitality
2. Vital, transforming worship
3. A focus on mission
4. Gifts and call as the basis for ministry
5. A commitment to equipping
6. Shared ministry and mission
7. Spirit-led organization
8. Holistic small groups
9. Commitment to evangelism and numerical growth

On a scale of 1–5, with 1 being "needs work" and 5 being "in good shape," how would you rank your congregation in each of these areas? A low score indicates a quality that is out of alignment. What steps could you take immediately to improve this quality? What are the long-term goals in this area, and will the immediate steps move you in that direction? Since we know everything is connected, what is something that you can draw on from an area of strength that will improve an area that needs work?

Connected and Connecting

Last year I designed and led a leadership retreat for a church in Moorestown, New Jersey. I had a delightful day with this group and planned what I anticipated would be a meaningful conclusion. We formed a large circle. I produced a large ball of yarn and explained that I would hold the end of the string, toss the ball to someone, and ask him or her to share something about his or her retreat experience. That person would keep hold of the string and toss the ball to another. We would repeat this until everyone had shared and we had formed a web of yarn across the circle. Then we would conclude by singing the familiar chorus "Bind Us Together." Only no one in the circle, including the music director, organist, pastor, and church and community choir members, knew this chorus.

We were connected, but we were not connecting. I had been in so many churches in recent years that had shifted to contemporary praise music or had blended the traditional with these choruses that I forgot there is still a strong tradition of excellent music that does not include these choruses. I was able to recover and propose we sing "Blest Be the Tie That Binds." Everyone knew this classic.

As a leader, it is important not only to see that everything is connected but also to connect everyone and find the points of connection with each one.

Reflection/Action

1. Physiology and ecclesiology merge in 1 Corinthians 12, where body parts are likened to gifts and ministries. On the anatomical chart of your church, what body part(s) are you most like?

2. Tape a large panel of newsprint or shelf paper to the wall. Draw a church building in the center of the paper and label it "The world of our church." Ask a significant group of church leaders and/or congregants to begin drawing, cutting and pasting pictures, or writing key words that show all of the ways the congregation is connected to the sacred and secular worlds. Reflect on the significance of what is drawn.

3. The Leadership Network describes four types of leaders: traditionalists, conservatives, progressives, and radicals. Do the descriptions in this chapter fit your experience? What is the chemistry of these groups interacting in your congregation? How do these insights reframe the way you interact with one another?

4. Following the directions in this chapter, rate your congregational health in each of the nine characteristics of a disciple-making congregation (see p. 100). What would be the advantages and disadvantages of working on the weaker areas and of working on the stronger areas as next steps?

Pastor Kim wasn't quite sure Elder Ed understood what she meant when
she said the vision statement needed some teeth in it.

Envision Purpose and Power
Habakkuk 2:2

If thou indeed derive thy light from Heaven,
Then, to the measure of that heaven-born light,
Shine, Poet! in thy place, and be content:—
—William Wordsworth, 1832

What You Need to Empower
1. Empower the people with purposeful vision.
2. Empower the church with prayerful discernment.
3. Empower yourself with a plan.

We were privileged to attend a staff meeting at Riverside Church in New York City. In that meeting, peace and justice were emphasized. One of my colleagues, also a guest at the meeting, asked about how they had decided peace would be on the agenda that day. Dr. James A. Forbes explained that before staff members get up every morning, they know that peace will be on the agenda of the church. Are you as clear about the purpose of your church? Before you get up each morning, do you know what vision keeps your church on course?

Empower the People with Purpose
Lacking a formally adopted statement, you may believe that your church does not have a purpose and vision. However, in the absence

of formal statements, there are always unstated and functional beliefs about purpose and vision. There may be as many different beliefs about vision and purpose as there are members, but more likely there are clusters of various understandings about purpose and vision. Sometimes these unstated understandings are at cross purposes. A helpful first step toward becoming a congregation empowered to change is to make explicit the unwritten and implicit beliefs people have about the mission and direction of the church.

Conduct a congregational survey, either in writing and solicited anonymously or in a meeting where members talk about the vision and purpose. Ask questions such as, What guides the church in its decision making? What is the primary purpose of the local church? You may collect a hodge-podge of answers to these questions, but look for the emerging points of agreement. Which answers echo each other? Which hint at common themes or priorities?

Then look for the disconnects between expressed beliefs and church practices. Do people believe that the purpose of the church is to win the lost but 95 percent of activities and budget are devoted to caring for the found? Do people believe that the vision is to develop mature disciples of Jesus Christ but there are no adult Sunday school classes, Bible studies, or small-group ministries?

Once you are able to articulate a kind of majority opinion on the purpose of the church and after you have assessed how effectively you are pursuing that purpose in your existing ministries, then you are ready for step two in the visioning process.

Empower the Church with Prayer

The first step focuses on the unwritten and implicit assumptions of the people and arrives at some kind of consensus. But the church that stops there makes a huge assumption; it assumes that where people want to be is where God is calling them to go. More often than not, that assumption is naïve presumption. Therefore, a second step is needed.

The second step is to take time to pray, study, discuss, and then discern a vision that is large enough to guide the church into the future. Take the past and present understandings that determine church priorities and policies and test them against what you discover in prayer and study. It is at this critical stage that you will either revert to a vision of a church as an end in itself or be stretched to think about the church as a means to an end that is God's reign. This is the shift from maintenance to ministry, from membership to mission; it is what is meant by "missional church."[1]

I am amazed when I ask church leaders who have a vision statement to recite it and they stumble. If you fall into that category, you may want to begin the visioning process afresh. A statement drafted by the pastor or crafted by a committee may contain wonderful sentiments and cause heads to nod in assent, but it will not be emotionally owned by the entire congregation. The goal is to involve the maximum number of persons in struggling with, shaping, and owning the vision. Don't be surprised or discouraged by the time and energy this process requires—not if the net result is an honest expression of what your congregation is passionate about doing and becoming.

At the end of this time of discernment, congregations often heave a great sigh of relief that they have done the hard and prayerful work of discerning a vision statement for the church of the twenty-first century and have clarified their purpose. The vision is printed on church bulletins and newsletters, embraced by the majority, and framed and hung conspicuously on the wall. However, the process is incomplete without an important third step.

Empower Yourself with a Plan

It is not enough to have a pretty vision statement framed and hanging in the church foyer. Churches need a vision path. How is the vision to become a reality? How will the church be intentional about living the vision? How will the church get from point A (where we are now) to point B (where the vision leads us)? Will the new vision be a plumb line against which future decisions are made? The vision path is the map that leads toward your vision.

It may appear that I have debunked vision and mission statements. I *am* critical of statements that are the "right answer" in much the same way that I despise when "Jesus" is always the right answer to any question in a children's sermon. Creating a statement is not a test of knowledge but a covenant of commitment that spiritually discerns the sacred and profane contexts and expresses an understanding of God's will for this moment.

Without effective leadership, the vision process often falls apart at this point—just when the vision needs to move forward. Strong leaders are persons with high personal standards that drive them to seek performance improvements for themselves and those they lead. They are pragmatic, setting measurable and challenging goals. They are able to calculate risk so that goals are worthy but attainable. A hallmark of achievement is continuously learning and teaching ways to do better.[2]

Another key to effective leadership is the area of emotional competency called *achievement drive*.[3] Without it, your vision and vision path may stall in the execution. "Execution" is a word with harsh connotations, but its origins are worth remembering: *ex sequi*, meaning "follow out." In other words, the ability to implement a plan and follow through will be a necessary discipline for any leader of congregational transformation. All of the pastors in our study had strengths in the emotional competencies of organizational awareness and inspiration. They were keenly aware of where their congregations were located in the present and able to move people with a compelling vision and inspire others to follow toward the future. They knew where points A and B were: where they were and where they wanted to go. What they lacked was the aptitude for making the transition from the present (A) to the preferred future (B) guided by purpose and vision. What they lacked were the qualities of execution and achievement.

Execution and achievement require some of the following:

1. Break the goal into pieces or steps that are attainable and morale-boosting as each is achieved.

2. Set benchmarks and deadlines (mileposts) and monitor progress. Know what needs to be done.

3. Learn from your mistakes; be flexible and adaptable when faced with obstacles and stress.

4. Trust your team and your leaders, and use their gifts.

5. Celebrate accomplishments along the way and link them to the vision.

6. Delegate responsibility for implementing each decision or plan.

7. Allocate adequate time and money to accomplish goals. (The plumb line of the vision statement can help prioritize limited resources.)

8. Equip leaders to succeed. Provide training, tools, and a support system.

The Power of Vision in Scripture

The prevalence of vision and mission statements in the corporate world and business literature can reduce the development of a church vision to an organizational "best practice." That would be a serious misunderstanding of biblical vision. Vision is inextricably linked with the Old Testament prophets in the Bible. Samuel, Nathan, Jeremiah, Isaiah, Daniel, Ezekiel, Obadiah, Micah, Nahum, and Habakkuk receive visions from God. The oft-quoted Proverbs 29:18, "Where there is no vision, the people perish" (KJV), can be translated "Where there is no prophecy, the people cast off all restraint" (NRSV). Other versions translate "vision" as "revelation." Receiving a vision is a holy transaction; vision is a word

107

from the Lord about the future. Jeremiah laments that Jerusalem's prophets obtain no vision from the Lord (Lamentations 2:9) and see false and deceptive visions (v. 14). It is paramount that the authors of a vision statement sort out their own preferences from God's. When the vision is clear, then the words of the prophet are God's words to us: "write the vision; make it plain . . . so that a runner may read it" (Habakkuk 2:2). Write it billboard size so that motorists speeding by can read it!

We know there are a lot of eloquent vision and mission statements in the Scriptures that floundered because God's people did not own them, wandering from the vision path or executing other plans. Mostly they separated their religious life from their political and moral lives. It is good to be reminded that the prophets of the Old Testament received visions in which faith and life were daily woven together and that New Testament prophets received visions that expanded their possibilities for ministry. Ananias and Saul were brought together by a vision (Acts 9:10-19). The Roman centurion Cornelius and Simon Peter were introduced by a vision (Acts 10:1-8). Peter was given a vision that included Gentiles (Acts 10:9-16). Paul changes his destination to Macedonia because of a vision (Acts 16:9). Vision brought new possibilities that shaped the early church and continues to guide it today.

Reflection/Action

1. We have domesticated the life-altering and nation-altering visions of the Bible. We take several steps away from persons who claim to have received visions from God. What are the preconditions for God sending a fresh vision, how do we know the vision is from God, and how do we prophetically announce this vision?

2. I raised the concern that mission and vision statements always be accompanied by a vision path. If your church does not have a recent statement, create a process for developing and advertising a

fresh vision of the purpose of your church. Listen and envision in small groups before a task force begins drafting a document. Remember to keep it short.

3. Begin the hard work of creating a vision path. Here is an excellent place to engage the creativity of many persons in the congregation. Include the perspectives of the conservatives, traditionalists, progressives, and radicals described in Step 9.

4. What have you or the church been procrastinating doing? Name it. What would it take to complete this and have the satisfaction of successfully executing a project? Who and what will be needed? Set benchmarks and timelines. Just do it.

Deacon Ron tested Pastor Linda's notion that no one
player is bigger than the whole team.

Coach and Be Coached
Acts 4:1-22

The toughest thing to "get" about coaching is just how relational it is. People ask me all the time to send them my curriculum on mentoring, and I keep thinking, that's like sending you my notes on "How to be a Friend."

—Steve Nicholson, *Coaching Church Planters*[1]

What You Need to Learn
1. Learn the nature of coaching.
2. Learn the types of coaches.
3. Learn from biblical coaches.

Recently, when I was handling a historical booklet given to me by an elderly church member, a yellowed letter dated December 13, 1899, fell out. It was addressed to the previous owner's Aunt Amanda, who had been one of the first women ever to be ordained by American Baptists in the nineteenth century. The letter was from a pastor in Port Dickinson, New York, and it recounted challenges encountered at a special church business meeting convened to discuss an invitation to Aunt Amanda to preach at some special meetings—a kind of revival series intended to help the church achieve a better state of religious life. The pastor reported limited financial and human resources to support the invitation and went on to confide his extreme discouragement. He had been trying for two years to help the church and confessed that he was ready to give it up and seek another field. He signed his letter, "Yours with a sorrowful heart." Where would the pastor of such a church turn for counsel? Where do pastors and church leaders today turn for help when they need counsel and encouragement?

We firmly established in Step 7 the risks and detriments of Lone Ranger leadership, and this step is a close corollary to that principle. A good leader needs a good coach—someone to encourage, sustain, and challenge you on the path of renewal. Who asks *you* the good questions, walks with you in setting goals and writing strategic plans, helps you look honestly at your current realities, brainstorms solutions with you, prods you to frame measurable steps, and does all of this within a high trust relationship?

The Nature of Coaching

When the practice of executive coaching first crossed over from the business world to the church world, it was denominational staff, parachurch consultants, and megachurch experts who were the skilled coaches. However, coaching skills aren't just for denominational folks any more. Pastors need to coach and be coached— become coaches of church members and welcome 360-degree coaching for themselves.

When I was pastor of the Old Cohansey Church in New Jersey, our area minister recruited a group of ministers who were interested in evangelism. The area minister wasn't the expert, the consultant, or the mentor. He acted as facilitator, allowing group members to find solutions and be intentional in evangelistic effort using the resources and experiences of the group members. We met monthly to develop strategies for each of our churches. Each month we reported on progress or obstacles, and then we solved problems, encouraged, and prayed for one another. Eventually we celebrated the successes God gave each of us. We didn't know it then, but we had been coaching one another. The coaching became 360 degrees because the feedback and support we offered came full circle.

One popular contemporary model that makes excellent use of coaching is the *FISH!* philosophy.[2] To Christians, it may sound like an evangelism program, but it is a business program designed to improve employee attitudes and performance, based on the philosophy established by the owner of Seattle's famous Pike Place Fish Market. The four simple principles of *FISH!* are Be there, Play, Make their day, and Choose your attitude. The sequel is *FISH! Sticks*, which deals with sustaining positive change through three simple commitments: Find it, Live it, and Coach it—"it" being each employee's personal vision of the business. It is the *FISH! Sticks* commitment to coaching that demands our focus here.

One of the keys to sustaining positive change in a business or ministry is identified as coaching. The entire crew of the Pike Place Fish Market, including the owner, coach one another about their performance and faithfulness to their philosophy. One of the keys to successful coaching is the permission to speak into one another's lives. This is a big shift for many church leaders. It involves an invitation to others to offer mutual accountability and feedback about how the vision and purpose of the church is being lived out. The shift assumes trust, interdependence, and a commitment to the overarching vision.

Achieving those things requires an awareness of the normal development of a small group. The stages are often called forming, storming, norming, and performing. In stage one, *forming*, members are compliant and dependent on the designated leader; they want the leader to make the decisions and don't usually become involved in significant work together. Author and speaker Susan Wheelan says you know you are in stage one when the leader asks a question and no one responds. In stage two, *storming*, the group members appear to be fighting and struggling with the leader about authority and seeking to assert their individuality. This time of struggle is a necessary step to becoming community. Wheelan says you know you are in stage two when you'd rather have all of your teeth pulled than go to the next meeting. In stage three, *norming*, there is increased clarity and consensus, cooperation is more evident, and trust and cohesion increase. You are in stage three when the group member who drove you crazy for weeks now makes you smile. Stage four, *performing*, is "in the zone." The team has an open communication structure in which all members participate and are heard. The team solves problems together and finds ways to make decisions that are participatory. Wheelan coins the word *unleadership* to describe the ways work is done by delegation, maximizing each member's gifts. This is the stage of work and productivity in which mutual coaching happens naturally and appropriately.[3]

Sensitivity to where your group is in these stages of development will allow you, as facilitator or as a peer group member, to be more effective in offering 360-degree coaching. You will be less likely to offer too much or too little, to rush or obstruct the group's progress. You also will be better positioned to receive the coaching of others.

The Types of Coaches

Having established the basic nature of coaching, it is important to note that there are five types of coaches. First are the *skilled and trained coaches*. These are similar to executive coaches in the business world because they have formal training from experts such as George Bullard and Jane Creswell (see appendix, "Coaching"). Bullard describes several types of professional coaches. "Content rich" coaching seeks to remake the leader or congregation in the image of a body of content. "Contextual" coaching seeks to remake the leader or congregation in the image of God consistent with the ministry setting. "Neutral" coaching is the purest form of coaching and seeks to remake the leader or congregation in light of the issues identified by those being coached.[4]

The second type of coach is the *mentor*. This is a wise person with rich experience who is like a spiritual director guiding you in the practice of ministry. The mentor coach helps people identify their unique strengths and weaknesses and tie them to their personal and career goals. The mentor's goals include helping others develop long-range goals and a plan for achieving those goals and linking all of this to their daily work. These coaches believe in the potential of others.[5] In *Coaching Church Planters*, Steve Nicholson and Jeff Bailey[6] describe these roles for a coach: thought provoker, awareness raiser, observer, and cheerleader. (They also include adviser and resourcer, but I really think that is a consultant role.) Mentor coaching does not give advice, except in crises, but it does offer accountability.

Third, there are *occasional coaches*. Organizations, like people, have blind spots (see the Johari Window in Step 2, Reflection/Action). Occasional coaches serve as invited outsiders who visit a church or ministry and report their impressions and observations. As outsiders they will immediately notice general clutter, outdated bulletin boards and literature, and the hard-to-find nursery, and then they make suggestions about dozens of little changes that might make a better impression on visitors and increase the likelihood of their returning. Community leaders can be occasional coaches, helping the church connect with the needs of the community.

Fourth are *mutual coaches*. These are the persons we work alongside in daily ministry, with whom we speak honestly and solicit reciprocal feedback. These coaches can be found in stage four performing groups (see p. 114). This kind of coach might approach an organization as a new pastor in the heartland did. He met with his church leaders, and they asked him what he wanted them to do. This had been the pattern of the former

Pastor-in-Chief. The new pastor turned that model upside down by asking where the leaders wanted to go and how they wanted to get there. He would help them achieve their vision and goals. He would be the coach.

Fifth and finally, there are *exemplar coaches*. These are leaders whose examples continually inform your leadership style. The powerful influence of these coaches transcends time and place. We may have never met these coaches personally, but our style, our values, our behaviors, and our ways of thinking have been deeply influenced by them. Perhaps the best exemplar coaches are found in the Scriptures.

Biblical Coaches

I was tempted to title this book *An Idiot's Guide to Congregational Transformation,* playing off not only the popular series for "dummies" but also Peter's and John's appearance before the Jewish Sanhedrin (Acts 4). The two apostles had been arrested following the healing of the lame man. Astounded by the boldness of their teaching and preaching, the rulers, elders, scribes, and high priest are amazed that these "were uneducated and ordinary men" (v. 13). The Greek words are *agrammatoi* and *idiotai. Agrammatoi* has been variously translated, but literally it means "unable to write." It is easy to see the relationship between this Greek word and the English word *grammar.* The Greek *idiotai* has been translated as "untrained," "ignorant," and "ordinary." Commentaries tell us that it has the sense of "layperson," an individual not educated in the rabbinical schools or trained in the Law,[7] but its transliterated similarity to the English word *idiot* is immediately apparent.

Peter and John were Galilean fishermen who lacked the degrees and certifications expected by the Jewish leaders, but they had the one essential qualification for ministry—they had been with Jesus. That qualified these ordinary men to be extraordinary exemplar coaches. That is the first critical lesson communicated by the model of biblical coaching: If God could use ordinary people to transform the first-century world, then God can use ordinary people to transform churches today.

The second lesson in biblical coaching is that change annoys some people. Peter and John were divinely appointed exemplar coaches, but the Jewish leaders were annoyed that the apostles were "proclaiming that in Jesus there is the resurrection of the dead" (Acts 4:2). In biblical times, it was the Sanhedrin that was annoyed by Christ and his gospel; they were the religious establishment of first-century Jerusalem. Who is the religious establishment in the United States today? Not the Sanhedrin but the Christian church, in all of its diverse denominational structures. Who is it that is threatened by change in the church, even when it is inspired by the teachings of Jesus and animated by the Holy Spirit? Resistance comes from the inside.

That brings us to the third lesson of biblical coaching: Renewal breaks in from the outside. In the first century, fishermen and tax collectors were turning the world upside down. The same is likely to be true today. Leaders of transformation may not be the usual suspects. Be open to God doing a new thing. A new convert in a very traditional (and stuck) Pennsylvania church noticed the large, empty church parking lot on Saturday mornings and the large number of neighborhood teens around the church. He proposed that the church sponsor a roller hockey team. He would work out the equipment, insurance, parental consent, and supervision issues. He asked the church to do three things: open the parking lot, drop by when the teens were playing, and host an awards dinner. This decision, agreed to cautiously, opened the door for many other positive changes.

The fourth lesson offered by the biblical coaches is, Don't get in the way of God's work. When Peter and John ministered in Christ's name, five thousand people heard the word of God and believed. The man who had been cured stood beside Peter and John before the council. The Sanhedrin could say nothing in opposition, confessed that a notable sign had been done through Peter and John that could not be denied, and eventually let them go with a warning because the people were praising God for what had happened.

The fifth and most outstanding coaching lesson from this story is found in the boldness of the apostles. Neither Peter nor John was daunted by being arrested. Without hesitation Peter told the religious rulers, "Let it be known . . . that this man is standing before you in good health by the name of Jesus Christ of Nazareth, whom you crucified, whom God raised from the dead" (Acts 4:10). When they were warned to speak and teach no more in the name of Jesus, Peter and John defiantly declared, "Whether it is right in God's sight to listen to you rather than to God, you must judge; for we cannot keep from speaking about what we have seen and heard" (vv. 19-20).

In Tom Bandy's book on coaching change, he contrasts professional leaders with leaders who are coaches.[8] Professionals are schooled, trained, and certified, while coaches are grown, mentored, and accepted. Professionals implement and manage programs, while coaches create environments to birth potential. I prefer to think of church leaders as coaches rather than professionals. When a hierarchical or authoritative relationship changes from one-way to mutual coaching, then coaching around mutually formed plans and agreed-on paths can develop.

Reflection/Action

1. The Bible and church history are filled with unlikely exemplar coaches. Who are your coaches from the past and in the present?

2. What would it take to live out the *FISH!* philosophy in your church? Focus on the 360-degree coaching, in which regular, constructive feedback is expected, invited, and welcomed.

3. At what stage of group development is your leadership team(s)? Is it a vision-casting or vision-implementation team? Do people want in or out of the team? Why? Is there a succession strategy—that is, an intentional effort to coach a new generation of leaders?

4. What are your stereotypes of coaching? What new understanding of coaching would advance the ministry of the church?

"Just send me over some bolts.
I've got enough nuts in this congregation."

STEP 12

Be Your Very Best
Matthew 9:16-17; Mark 2:19-22; Luke 5:36-39

If God left some things contingent on man's thinking and working, why may he not have left some things contingent on man's praying? The testimony of the great souls is a clear affirmative to this: some things never without thinking; some things never without working; some things never without praying! Prayer is one of the three forms of man's cooperation with God.

—Harry Emerson Fosdick,
The Meaning of Prayer[1]

What You Need to Improve
1. Improve your knowledge of demographics.
2. Improve your use of marketing and advertising.
3. Improve your tools for assessment.

The Cuban pastor whispered to me that local government officials had arrived at their midweek service of prayer and Bible study and bulldozed their church building. They were being made an example because they had built an addition to their edifice without the proper permits. Permits for painting, renovating, or building churches are seldom issued in Cuba. However, the parsonage remained standing, and there are no similar regulations or restrictions about improving parsonages. So the congregation enlarged the parsonage and moved their services to that spacious building.

Practical challenges to building God's house are ancient. After the Babylonians bulldozed Solomon's temple, fifty thousand Israelites returned from captivity intent on restoring the fallen temple (Ezra 2). They built an altar in the seventh month and laid a foundation in the second year. Then construction was suspended by order of the Persian king. Building resumed in the time of Haggai and Zechariah, when a later Persian ruler, King Darius, granted permission.

Church under Construction

The challenges to improving or transforming your church are not limited to the practical obstacles to enlarging a physical structure. There are also the challenges of implementing twenty-first-century ministry tools in the service of a first-century Christian faith. Consider how the traditional Christmas pageant has been transformed with elaborate light shows, huge sound systems, live animals, and other special effects. It also raises the question of how to draw the line between flashy entertainment and substantial evangelism and discipleship. Is it legitimate to attempt reaching a lost world for Christ through the means of pop culture's tools?

My New Testament professor, in his German accent, constantly distinguished between husk and kernel in Scripture. The husk is the container, the first-century political, social, linguistic, and religious context. The kernel is Jesus' life and message. We often debate what happens when the husk is a twenty-first-century container, but Jesus also encountered a clash between his culture and God's kingdom values.

Jesus told parables to illustrate the dilemma. The message of those parables was simple: new cloth patched on an old garment will shrink and tear away. New wine in old brittle wineskins will ferment, stretching the skin to the breaking point, and spilling the wine. Some of Jesus' methods employed traditional wineskins—the parables and question-and-answer styles of teaching were part of first-century Jewish culture. However, much of the content of his teaching was new wine—and it required new methods that challenged his culture. He enlisted ordinary men as his disciples; he included women in his company; he broke with the legalism of the Pharisees; his pulpit could be a seashore or mountainside as well as the synagogue, and he called his hearers away from the husk of tradition and back to the kernel of God's truth and grace.

The Christian church has followed the example of its founder. Throughout history, we preserved the kernel of the gospel message while regularly employing a new husk. The early church replaced scrolls with books and the hereditary priesthood with charismatic leaders. The medieval church used visual art to tell the old, old story to illiterate Europeans. The Renaissance church used the printing press to spread the Word. In the nineteenth century, churches used the railroad and automobiles to evangelize and plant churches. In the twentieth century, Christians embraced the new technologies of radio and television. The twenty-first century offers us animated billboards, iPods, the Internet, satellite downlinks, franchise churches, and postmodern apologetics and polity.

Pursue Excellence—in Your Own Way

There are more than twelve hundred megachurches in the United States. Many were founded to attract baby boomers who expect excellence. The off-key choir, amateur organist, nursery with used baby furniture, lectors whose tongues trip over biblical names, and inhospitable greeters and ushers are unacceptable. The reasoning was simple: doesn't God deserve our best? Absolutely. But somewhere along the way "*our* very best" became confused with "*the* very best," and churches everywhere strived to imitate the megachurches. But at what cost?

Marilyn was born with Down syndrome and became a high-functioning adult, able to read at an elementary level, work at a local nursing home, and play the clarinet. She was a bad clarinet player by the standards of the world but an excellent clarinet player *by God's standards*. On an occasional Sunday, Marilyn was the "special music," and her testimony and music were appreciated as if she were Pete Fountain. Paul introduces his "love chapter" to the Corinthians by writing, "And I will show you a still more excellent way" (1 Corinthians 12:31). The excellence God calls us to is love of God, neighbor, one another (other Christians), and even our enemies. The same kind of love that God has for the world.

The power of the ordinary church—and I use that adjective in the sense of ordinary believers (Acts 4:13)—is that God chose the foolish, weak, low, and despised (1 Corinthians 1:26-31). God *does* expect our very best—but that is based on the gifts, talents, resources, skills, and knowledge God has given us. This is true for individuals and for congregations, so don't retro-fit your church to be seeker-sensitive, GenX-friendly, or postmodern-emergent for the wrong reasons. Be authentic, be excellent according to your God-given potential, and be "lovely" so the world might say, "See how they love one another."

Do not misunderstand me. Practical transformation tools are necessary to building up the church and expanding the kingdom of God, but they are the least important thing in congregational transformation. This step is last because tools without the right craftsperson and the right building materials will result in a shoddy structure. But there *are* useful tools that will contribute to the construction of a more excellent church—and implemented correctly, they will help your congregation become the very best that God has called *you* to be. This chapter is about the tools of the renewal trade. However, the temptation is to reorganize when the right use of any time-tested tool or structure will work—and the wrong use of the novel and new will fail.

One qualification before we continue: If you do not have a computer with Internet access, you will find much of the toolkit frustrating. The computer has become a critical tool for ministry in the twenty-first century. A basic computer and Internet connection is within the financial reach of almost every church and pastor. If that is not the case for you, there are typically computers in the public library, in local schools, and in the homes and businesses of church members. Become familiar with the technology and discover the resources available online, particularly as it relates to the critical toolkit categories of demographics, marketing, and assessment.

Knowledge of Demographics

A suburban Philadelphia church asked me to do some demographic research. I looked at the census tract data for one mile around the church and for increments up to a five-mile radius. I took my camera and did a windshield survey. That is, I simply drove through the community and took pictures of places that offered insights and opportunities for ministry. The facts of my report dispelled a widely held belief that there were not many children or youth in the neighborhood.

Do it yourselfers can go to the U.S. Census website (www.census.gov) and click on American FactFinder for their zip code and find information on population, race and ethnicity, age, household, home ownership, education, income, and disabilities. If you burrow deeper on the census and block tracts, you can uncover details such as commuting times and distances to work and hundreds of facts on thematic maps and demographic profiles.

Those who want more help can purchase information from services such as Percept. Percept's demographic information comes from four sources, both government and private. Percept offers mission and ministry planning from less than $100 for a summary of a zip code area to thousands of dollars for complex analysis of neighborhoods. Visit www.percept1.com or contact them at

Percept, 29889 Santa Margarita Parkway, Rancho Santa Margarita, CA 92688-3609 (800-442-6277 or 949-635-1282).

A second source for demographic information is Visions-Decisions: Demography for Churches. Their Unchurched/Churched Index shows rates of affiliation. Their Religious Preference Index shows religious leanings in your area. Their National Church Database shows the churches in your community and their theological bent, denomination, race/ethnicity, and membership size. They offer congregational and on-site studies. Visit visions-decisions.com or contact them at Visions-Decisions, P.O. Box 94144, Atlanta, GA 30377 (800-524-1445).

The Association of Religion Data Archives (ARDA) is a third source of help with local and national information. They offer a Community Profile Builder, provide general information on religion in America (350 surveys), and have a helpful tool for organizing U.S. Census data and other free public information. Here is a place to find MOSAIC Cluster descriptions. MOSAIC is a geodemographic segmentation system developed by Experian (the credit report people) and marketed in more than twenty countries. The basic premise of geodemographic segmentation is that people tend to gravitate toward communities with other people of similar backgrounds, interests, and means.

Use of Marketing and Advertising

Have you ever said, "Our church is one of the best-kept secrets. What can we do?" If so, then you have a marketing concern. Marketing tools take many forms. Churches have become a large niche market, and there are companies and consultants to help with logos and branding, direct mail, signs and banners, websites, videos, and slide downloads. Church marketers emphasize that marketing is not the same as advertising and remind us that we have the greatest story ever told, but people need to hear it. Marketing is identifying who you are as a church and determining how to communicate that message to those who need to be a part of the church. "One of the church's greatest shortcomings is a failure to market itself authentically. . . . You've seen the typos, bad clip art, poor layouts. It's easy to do marketing badly. But there's also the tendency toward airbrushed perfection, pressed suits and coiffed hair and multicultural pictures that don't match the Sunday morning reality. Seemingly professional marketing can be just as bad as the unprofessional type."[2]

Thinking in terms of customers and markets, however, might not always bring out the best in a church leader, according to Jackson Carroll, professor emeritus of religion and society and former director of research at the Pulpit & Pew Project at Duke University in Durham, North Carolina. He cites the example of Southern preachers who took up the cause of civil rights in the 1960s despite vehement local resistance. "It didn't help marketing at all," Professor Carroll says. "People left churches in droves when pastors or leaders in the congregation took a strong stand in favor of integration, [but] they did it anyway." Today, he says, pastors who make marketing a top priority run the risk of fostering "a congregation that refuses to deal with issues of individual or social justice because it might offend someone."[3]

Online searches about church marketing and advertising will yield lots of hits. I recommend four sites: Church Marketing Sucks, Church Ad Project, Outreach, Inc., and Religion Communicators Council. Church Marketing Sucks (www.churchmarketing sucks.com) is a blog from the Center for Church Communication (www.cfcclabs.com) full of helpful hints for churches on best practices for church marketing.

The Church Ad Project (www.churchad.com) offers advertising tools for evangelism such as posters, postcards, door hangers, radio spots, and direct mail. The Church Ad Project's *Advertising the Local Church*[4] is in its sixth edition. The topics range from advertising as evangelism to the use of direct mail.

Outreach, Inc. (www.outreach.com) offers bulletins, banners, logos, and other tools for outreach. They have been very creative in connecting popular culture with outreach tools (postcards, sermons, books, evangelism strategies). Recently they have created resources for Mel Gibson's *Passion of the Christ,* C. S. Lewis's *Chronicles of Narnia,* and Dan Brown's *DaVinci Code* that coincided with the release of the movies.

The Religion Communicators Council (www.religioncommunicators.org) is an interfaith association of communicators working in print and electronic communication, marketing, and public relations. They have produced *Speaking Faith: The Essential Handbook for Religious Communicators.*[5] Here you will find help with writing press releases, graphic design, PowerPoint, crisis communications, broadcasting worship, copyright, consultants, and dozens of other practical topics.

Tools for Assessment

Assessment tools can be helpful at the beginning of a transformation journey to measure readiness, to benchmark the current church realities, or to explore opportunities for growth and outreach. George Bullard has developed an initial assessment tool to see if a congregation is ready for change and transition. The tool can be found at www.congregationalresources.org in the article "Is Your Congregation Ready for Change and Transition Leading to Transformation?"[6]

The Hartford Institute for Religious Research (HIRR) has several assessment inventories. The Church Planning Inventory and Parish Profile Inventory are available online (hirr.hartsem.edu). The website links to four large national studies that allow you to view your congregation in comparison with other churches.[7] The Congregational Studies Project Team of HIRR publishes an excellent resource book, *Studying Congregations: A New Handbook.*[8] It provides techniques for studying the congregation as well as a framework for understanding the nature of the congregation. The HIRR forte is sociology of religion, and you will find links to Barna Group (www.barna.org), The Alban Institute (www.alban.org),

Leadership Network (www.leadnet.org), and Adherents.com (www.adherents.com), which is a treasure trove of statistical information on 4,500 denominations and world religions.

One of the largest studies of healthy churches is Christian Schwartz's study of one thousand congregations. His research is the basis for Natural Church Development.[9] The eight qualities are empowering leadership, gift-oriented ministry, passionate spirituality, functional structures, inspiring worship, holistic small groups, need-oriented evangelism, and loving relationships. None of these qualities can be absent and must be present in a "minimum factor" for congregational health. The Implementation Guide gives instructions on how to conduct the NCD survey and guides a church through developing a strategy to address the minimum factors.

Phillip Alessi applies the NCD principles to new church planting.[10] A church seeking transformation might do well to pay attention to his new church planting approach. The weakness of Natural Church Development is the inward focus on the church, as if congregational health were an end in itself. Healthy churches journey inward to prepare for the journey outward. Missional action, not functional structures, is the last step in assembling a healthy church.

General Ministry Resources

I want to recommend additional tools for general information about congregational transformation. The *40 Days of Purpose* campaign (www.purposedriven.com) coming out of Rick Warren's Saddleback Church combines the journey inward with the journey outward. This intensive, church-wide spiritual growth campaign commissions believers to fulfill their unique, God-appointed mission to the world. A Mission Fair during weekend five gets the church members outside of the four walls and into the local community to express love and good works in tangible ways.

NET Results: New Ideas in Church Vitality (www.netresults.org), mentioned earlier, was founded by Herb Miller as a ministry of the

Christian Church (Disciples of Christ). It publishes a monthly journal and provides consultation, conferences, and online seminars.

The Center for Parish Development (www.missionalchurch.org), founded by Paul Dietterich, offers resources, seminars, and consulting on the missional church. The distinction between a church with a mission and a missional church is significant. A church with a mission often sends others to witness on its behalf. A missional church understands that the congregation itself is sent by God to proclaim and be a sign of the reign of God.

The Alpha Course (www.alphausa.org) is a ten-week course that introduces seekers to the basics of Christianity. The format is a meal, talk, and small-group discussion. A retreat is planned midway through the course, and participants are introduced to the work of the Holy Spirit and given an opportunity to make a decision to follow Jesus. Thousands of Alpha courses are now running in many countries, and the material has been translated into many different languages. There are courses for youth, college students, prisoners, military, and workplaces.

There are many online spiritual gift inventories (see appendix, "Spiritual Gifts"). Some include the preternatural gifts of the Spirit. All of the spiritual gift inventories stress that spiritual gifts are not just a matter of self-identification but need to be coupled with the affirmation of the community. It is not enough to think that I have the spiritual gift of preaching; it is important that the congregation recognize and affirm that gift.

As I conclude, I am reminded of Johan Sebastian Bach, the patron saint of church musicians. It is well known that he signed his works *Soli Deo Gloria,* "To God alone, the glory" at the conclusion of his compositions. I recently learned that he was often in the habit of writing the words *Jesus Juva,* "Help me, Jesus," on the paper before he started. The faithful manner in which we start our work is just as important as the conclusion. May Bach's music and witness inspire all our transformational ministries!

APPENDIX

Tool Kit

For each general topic that follows, resources and questions to consider are given. Unless otherwise indicated, all resources may be ordered through the publisher or from standard online retailers, such as amazon.com, christianbooks.com, or bn.com.

Spiritual Gifts
Questions to Consider
1. What are your spiritual gifts, those of church leaders and members?
2. How are you and others using spiritual gifts in ministry?
3. How is gift discernment incorporated into the disciple-making ministry of your church?
4. How do you nurture the gifts of the people so that they mature into skilled ministers?

Suggested Resources
Brown, Patricia D. *Spirit Gifts: One Spirit, Many Gifts*. Abingdon, 1996. Leader's resources and participant's workbook.

Bryant, Charles V. *Rediscovering Our Spiritual Gifts: Building Up the Body of Christ through the Gifts of the Spirit*. Upper Room Books, 1991.

Dave Ray, Wake Up! You Have A Ministry. Core Ministries, 2000.

Griend, Alvin J. Vander. *Discover Your Gifts: And Learn How to Use Them*. CRC Publications, 1996. Rev. ed. Leader's guide and student manual.

Wagner, C. Peter. *Discover Your Spiritual Gifts*. Regal Books, 2005.

Spiritual and Relational Vitality
Questions to Consider
1. What proportion of your church members and attendees participate in intentional spiritual disciplines?
2. How many are part of a small group that addresses spiritual maturing?
3. How do you evaluate the spiritual maturity of church leaders?
4. How does your church deal with conflict? (Do you bury conflict in the belief

that real Christians don't fight or disagree? Do you say and do hostile things to each other? Do you split?)

5. In what ways do you use conflict as an opportunity to open up and share what matters most?

6. What training have you had in conflict transformation?

Suggested Resources

Friend, Howard E., Jr. *Recovering the Sacred Center: Church Renewal from the Inside Out.* Judson Press, 1998.

Morris, Danny E., and Charles M. Olsen. *Discerning God's Will Together: A Spiritual Practice for the Church.* Upper Room Books, 1997.

Nouwen, Henri J. M. *Bread for the Journey: A Daybook of Wisdom and Faith.* Harper San Francisco, 1997.

Palmer, Parker J. *The Courage to Teach: Exploring the Inner Landscape of a Teacher's Life.* Jossey-Bass, 1998.

Weavings (bimonthly journal from The Upper Room). To subscribe, call 800-925-6847 or visit www.upperroom.org/weavings.

Adult Personal Conflict Style Inventory (peace.mennolink.org/resources/conflict style). An online survey to determine your preferred method of conflict resolution, plus group exercises and training methods.

Coaching

Questions to Consider

1. When have you been coached? What were the characteristics of your coach(es)?

2. In what circumstances have you invited feedback (coaching) from peers, congregants, or supervisors?

3. Which coaching experiences have been in support of mastering a skill or knowledge versus in support of discovering goals, purposes, and potential? How do those types of coaching differ?

4. What do you think is necessary to improve the 360-degree coaching environment of the church—i.e., to make mutual coaching a natural part of congregational life?

Suggested Resources

Creswell, Jane. *Christ-centered Coaching: Seven Benefits for Ministry Leaders.* St. Louis: Lake Hickory Resources. 2006.

ILS (in liminal space) Coaching and Consulting. Founded by Brian McLaren. www.ilscc.net.

Lake Hickory Training and Resource Center. Lake Hickory, North Carolina. Coaching center run by George Bullard (www.hollifield.org/valwood) and Jane Creswell (www.internal-impact.com).

TOOL KIT

Worship
Questions to Consider
1. Describe the normal worship experience in your church.
2. Do the words you use to describe worship suggest life, vibrancy, enthusiasm, and depth?
3. What worship resources do you use in preparing and carrying out worship?
4. How frequently do the worship leaders in your congregation go to training events to expand their skills and awareness of trends?
5. Who participates in planning and leading worship? Clergy and laity? Adults and youth? Is youth participation only on Youth Sunday?
6. Describe worship experiences in your church beyond the regular Sunday morning service.
7. How and where do you include teaching about worship in your discipling process?

Suggested Resources
Berglund, Brad. *Reinventing Sunday: Breakthrough Ideas for Transforming Worship*. Judson Press, 2001. Also see the author's website, www.reinventing sunday.com and *Reinventing Worship: Prayers, Readings, Special Services, and More*. Judson Press, 2006. Includes a CD-ROM containing all worship resources included in the book.

Bonn, Linda. *The Work of the Worship Committee*. Judson Press, 1998.

Dawn, Marva. *Reaching Out without Dumbing Down: A Theology of Worship for This Urgent Time*. Eerdmans, 1995.

Doran, Carol, and Thomas H. Troeger. *Trouble at the Table: Gathering the Tribes for Worship*. Abingdon, 1992.

Gaddy, C. Welton, and Don W. Nixon. *Worship: A Symphony for the Senses*. Smyth & Helwys, 1995.

Liesch, Barry. *The New Worship: Straight Talk on Music and the Church*. Baker, 1996.

Ng, David, and Virginia Thomas. *Children in the Worshiping Community*. John Knox Press, 1981.

Webber, Robert E. *Worship Old and New*. Zondervan, 1982. Also see the author's website, www.ancientfutureworship.com.

Websites
Questions to Consider
1. How do you use the Internet (e.g., research, exploration, images for worship or communication, etc.)?
2. A Google search on "congregational transformation" yields 385,000 results. Have you considered using this largely free resource as an aid to church renewal? Why or why not?

3. The stress and challenges of transformation may be reduced with creativity and humor. Try searching the Web by combining key words such as "humor" and "creative" with "congregational transformation."

4. Consider how you might weave the twelve steps of this book with images and ideas discovered on the Internet and your own congregational photos into a digital PowerPoint presentation. What would it take to create such a presentation? Identify someone with the skills and resources to create it, and consider how best it could be used to challenge your congregation.

Suggested Resources

www.amahoro.info — an emergent church website.

www.anewkindofchristian.com — the website for Brian McLaren's book, *A New Kind of Christian.*

www.emergentvillage.com — featuring a postmodern viewpoint.

www.resourcingchristianity.org — Resources for American Christianity website, administered by the Lilly Endowment.

www.newadvent.org — a 12,000+ entry encyclopedia with a fair and objective presentation.

www.theooze.com — an edgy emergent-church website offering postmodern approaches to church renewal.

www.transformingchurch.com/resourcetoolbox — a partnership of the Academy for Congregational Transformation and the Evangelical Lutheran Church of America Southeastern Synod's Commission for Transforming Congregations.

Mission

Questions to Consider

1. What proportion of your church members participate in hands-on mission activities or events?

2. What are you doing to increase that number?

3. How many members would you like to see involved?

4. How does your church describe the budget process—money language or mission language?

5. How do you help people move from giving money and things to engaging with people who need ministry?

6. How do you measure the growth from giving money and things to engagement with people?

Suggested Resources

Clegg, Tom, and Warren Bird. *Lost in America: How You and Your Church Can Impact the World Next Door.* Group Publishing, 2001.

Hauck, Kenneth. *Christian Caregiving: A Way of Life; The Heart of Stephen Ministry* (VHS). Available at www.stephenministries.org.

Mission Comes Alive! A handbook of mission education for the local church. Revised by James G. Layton. American Baptist Churches, USA, 1997. To order, call 800-ABC-3USA, ext. 2464, or visit www.nationalministries.org.

Sider, Ronald, Heidi Rolland-Unruh, and Philip Olson. *Churches That Make a Difference—Reaching your Community with Good News and Good Works.* Baker, 2002.

Slaughter, Michael. *Out on the Edge: A Wake-up Call for Church Leaders on the Edge of the Media Reformation.* Abingdon, 1998.

Discipleship

Questions to Consider

1. How do you use continuing education funds?
2. Is there a budget line for continuing education funds?
3. Who seeks learning opportunities for those being asked to serve?
4. Who recruits people to be equipped for ministry?
5. Describe the disciple-making curriculum in your church. Does it include Bible study, spiritual disciplines, evangelism skills, and specialized skills for ministries?

Suggested Resources

Bowdon, Boyce A. *The Child-Friendly Church: 150 Models of Ministry with Children.* Abingdon, 1999.

Chism, Keith A. *Christian Education for the African American Community: Teacher Training in the Black Church.* Discipleship Resources, 1996.

Galindo, Israel. *The Craft of Christian Teaching: Essentials for Becoming a Very Good Teacher.* Judson Press, 1998.

Hunt, Josh, with Larry Mays, *Disciple-Making Teachers: How to Equip Adults for Growth and Action.* Vital Ministry, 1999.

Isham, Linda R. *Embracing the Future: A Guide for Reshaping Your Church's Teaching Ministry.* Judson Press, 1999.

Pathways: Fostering Spiritual Growth among At-Risk Youth (a Boys Town Training Program) and *The Ongoing Journey, Awakening Spiritual Life in At-Risk Youth.* Available from Boys Town Press, 14100 Crawford St, Boys Town, NE 68010, by calling 800-282-6657, or visiting www.girlsandboystown.org/products/booksvideos/btpress.htm.

"The Work of the Church" series, including titles on the trustee, clerk, treasurer, deaconess, pastoral relations committee, Sunday school superintendent, usher, worship committee, and more. To order, call Judson Press at 800-458-3766.

Yount, Christine. *Recruit and Nurture Awesome Volunteers for Children's Ministry.* Group Publishing, 1998.

Evangelism and Numerical Growth
Questions to Consider
1. In planning your local mission engagement, how does your congregation talk about opportunities for evangelism?
2. What training for identifying and developing evangelism gifts does your church provide when that spiritual gift is discerned in a member?
3. How do your church's spiritual growth ministries, including Christian education, equip members for evangelism?
4. How do you prepare and encourage members to speak authentically and clearly about the gospel? Specifically, how do the leaders of your church practice and model evangelism?

Suggested Resources
Arn, Win, and Charles Arn. *The Master's Plan for Making Disciples*. Second ed. Baker, 1998.
Boursier, Helen. *Tell It with Style: Evangelism for Every Personality Type*. InterVarsity Press, 1995.
Mittelberg, Mark. *Becoming a Contagious Church*. Zondervan, 2000.

Shared Ministry and Mission
Questions to Consider
1. Describe how your church decides who does what.
2. How many laypersons are engaged in what we have in the past thought of as "the minister's job"?
3. How many members have gone through a gift discovery process?
4. What is the pastor's primary role in the church?
5. How much time and encouragement do you give leaders to take personal spiritual retreats or other deepening of his or her spiritual life?

Suggested Resources
Gangel, Kenneth. *Coaching Ministry Teams: Leadership and Management in Christian Organizations*. Word, 2000.
Holderness, Ginny Ward. *Teaming Up: Shared Leadership in Youth Ministry*. Westminster/John Knox Press, 1997.
Howe, Leroy. *A Pastor in Every Pew: Equipping Laity for Pastoral Care*. Judson Press, 2000.
Woods, C. Jeff. *Better Than Success: Eight Principles of Faithful Leadership*. Judson Press, 2001.

Spirit-Led Organization
Questions to Consider
1. What percentage of members serves on committees, boards, or other groups?

2. What percentage of members is engaged in mission outside the doors of the church?
3. When did you last change the constitution and bylaws to reflect a focus on mission?
4. How long does it take for a new proposal for mission to gain approval?

Suggested Resources
Buchan, Jim. *Walking the Leadership Highway Without Becoming Roadkill.* Smyth & Helwys, 2005.
Herrington, Jim, R. Robert Creech, and Trisha Taylor. *The Leader's Journey: Accepting the Call to Personal and Congregational Transformation.* Jossey-Bass, 2003.
Ott, Stephen. *Twelve Dynamic Shifts.* Eerdmans, 2002.
Phillips, Mark. *Help! My Church Is Growing.* Smyth & Helwys, 2005.
Vander Griend, Alvin J., with Edith Bajema. *The Praying Church Sourcebook.* Church Development Resources, 1997.

Small Groups
Questions to Consider
1. How many small groups do you have in your church?
2. What is the focus of small groups in your church?
3. What percentage of your members participates in small groups?
4. What training do you provide for small-group leaders?
5. What ongoing mentoring or coaching do you provide for small-group leaders?

Suggested Resources
Bandy, Thomas. *Christian Chaos: Revolutionizing the Congregation.* Abingdon, 1999.
Castellanos, César. *Successful Leadership Through the Government of G12.* G12 Editors, 2003.
Corrigan, Thom. *Small Group Fitness Kit.* NavPress, 1996. To order, call Judson Press at 800-458-3766.
Donahue, Bill. *Leading Life-Changing Small Groups.* Zondervan, 1996.
Frazee, Randy. *The Connecting Church: Beyond Small Groups.* Zondervan, 2001.
Galindo, Israel. *How to Be the Best Christian Study Group Leader Ever in the Whole History of the Universe.* Judson Press. 2006.
Hestenes, Roberta. *Using the Bible in Groups.* Westminster/John Knox. 1985.
Sheely, Steve. *Leader's Handbook for Small Groups.* Serendipity House. 1994. To order, call Serendipity House at 800-525-9563.
Turner, Nathan W. *Leading Small Groups: Basic Skills for Church and Community Organizations.* Judson Press. 1997.

NOTES

Introduction

1. David G. Dethmers, *Revive Us Again! Hope for Stagnant, Stuck, and Sterile Churches* (New York: Reformed Church Press, 1994).

2. Kenneth A. Halstead, *From Stuck to Unstuck: Overcoming Congregational Impasse* (Washington, D.C.: The Alban Institute, 1998), 2.

3. Statistics listed online at http://www.newchurchinitiatives.org/morechurches/index.htm (accessed February 23, 2006).

4. *The Big Book*, 4th ed. (New York: Alcoholics Anonymous World Services, Inc., 2001), 59–60.

5. Thomas G. Bandy's *Kicking Habits: Welcome Relief for Addicted Churches* (Nashville: Abingdon, 1997) is a provocative book that uses the language of addiction and recovery to help churches thrive.

Step 1

1. Robert D. Dale, *To Dream Again: How to Help Your Church Come Alive* (Nashville: Broadman, 1981), 17.

2. George Barna, *Turn-Around Churches: How to Overcome Barriers to Growth and Bring New Life to an Established Church* (Ventura, Calif.: Regal Books, 1993), 19–23.

3. Loren B. Mead, *The Once and Future Church: Reinventing the Congregation for a New Mission Frontier* (Washington, D.C.: The Alban Institute, 1991), 25–29.

4. In this book, I refer frequently to the emergent church. The emergent church is a diffuse movement concerned about the deconstruction and reconstruction of Protestant Christianity in a postmodern cultural context. See Brian D. McLaren, *A Generous Orthodoxy* (Grand Rapids: Zondervan, 2004). McLaren's impossible subtitle, "Why I am a missional + evangelical + post/protestant + liberal/conservative + mystical/poetic + biblical + charismatic/contemplative + fundamentalist/calvinist + anabaptist/anglican + methodist + catholic + green + incarnational + depressed-yet-hopeful + emergent + unfinished Christian" says much about the movement. For a quick history, check Wikipedia, the free online encyclopedia, at http://en.wikipedia.org/wiki/Emerging _church.

5. McLaren, 31.

6. James F. Hopewell, *Congregation: Stories and Structures* (Philadelphia: Fortress, 1987), 193.

NOTES

Step 2

1. Explanation of answers: 1. Crosses and other symbols would be out of place in the plain meeting houses of the dissenter and separatist sects. 2. Stained-glass windows would evoke the Roman Catholic and Anglican traditions rejected by early Baptists. 3. Organ music would be unwelcome for another century. 4. Hymns would not be widely accepted until the 1800s. The early American churches sang psalms and scriptural songs. 5. Sunday schools were not founded until 1780. 6. Wine was commonly used until the temperance movement in the nineteenth century. 7. The Pilgrims and other New Englanders used the Geneva translation. 8. The modern missionary movement did not begin until the early nineteenth century. 9. Colonial churches were supported with pew rents, lotteries, and "subscriptions." 10. Alas, indoor plumbing was still missing from many church buildings well into the twentieth century. 11. Many of the early clergy were educated at universities in England. Roger Williams, founder of the First Baptist Church of America, was Cambridge-educated and proficient in Latin, Greek, and Hebrew. 12. They did not erect their first meetinghouse until 1700, sixty-two years after their founding. Many early churches met in barns, school-houses, and homes.

2. Jim Collins, *From Good to Great: Why Some Companies Make the Leap . . . and Others Don't* (New York: HarperBusiness, 2001), 168.

3. William M. Easum, "How to Address the Stress Points in Turnaround Churches." *NET Results* 27, no. 1 (January/ February 2006): 9–10.

4. George Barna, *Turn-Around Churches: How to Overcome Barriers to Growth and Bring New Life to an Established Church* (Ventura, Calif.: Regal Books, 1993), 47.

5. Robert D. Dale, *To Dream Again: How to Help Your Church Come Alive* (Nashville: Broadman, 1981), 5.

6. Derek J. Tidball, *Builders and Fools: Leadership in the Bible Way* (Leicester: InterVarsity Press, 1999).

7. E.g., Clementia, *The Epistle of Clement to James*, Ante-Nicene Fathers, 7:220–21.

8. The other classic texts that describe the gifts of the Spirit are Romans 12:3-8; Ephesians 4:11-12; 1 Peter 4:7-11. One of the best theological treatments of these lists as spiritual gifts rather than church offices is Miroslav Volf, *Work in the Spirit* (Eugene, Ore.: Wipf and Stock, 2001).

9. Quoted in Larry C. Spears and Michele Lawrence, eds., *Focus on Leadership: Servant-Leadership for the 21st Century* (New York: John Wiley and Sons, 2002), 19–20.

10. Joseph Luft and Harry Ingham, "The Johari Window: A Graphic Model of Interpersonal Awareness," *Proceedings of the Western Training Laboratory in Group Development* (Los Angeles: UCLA, 1955).

NOTES

Step 3

1. William M. Easum and Thomas G. Bandy, *Growing Spiritual Redwoods* (Nashville: Abingdon, 1997), 197. Used by permission.

2. Peter Scazzero, *The Emotionally Healthy Church: A Strategy for Discipleship That Actually Changes Lives* (Grand Rapids: Zondervan, 2003), 20. Scazzero has developed an Emotional/Spiritual Health Inventory that benchmarks where you are as a healthy leader (60–66).

3. William M. Easum, *Sacred Cows Make Gourmet Burgers: Ministry Anytime, Anywhere, by Anyone* (Nashville: Abingdon, 1995), 75. Used by permission.

4. Jim Collins, *From Good to Great: Why Some Companies Make the Leap . . . and Others Don't* (New York: Harper Business, 2001), 65.

5. A good introduction is Otto Kroeger and Janet M. Thuesen, *Type Talk: The 16 Personality Types That Determine How We Live, Love, and Work* (New York: Dell, 1988).

6. M. Robert Mulholland, Jr., *Invitation to a Journey: A Road Map for Spiritual Formation* (Downers Grove, Ill.: Inter-Varsity Press, 1993), 49–73.

7. Holy Resurrection Russian Orthodox Church was founded in 1794 by missionary monks from Valaam Monastery of the St. Petersburg diocese in Russia. Father Herman continued the work with the Alutiiq people for forty-three years. The nearby St. Herman's Theological Seminary is named in his honor.

8. For an introduction to the eleven powerful skills I learned and continue to use and teach, see John S. Savage, *Listening and Caring Skills: A Guide for Groups and Leaders* (Nashville: Abingdon, 1996). For additional information about training, visit www.leadplus.com.

9. Scazzero, 110–31. The prayer (excerpted here) can be found in its entirety at www.solinger.com/prayer.

10. Jim Collins, *Good to Great and the Social Sectors: A Monograph to Accompany Good to Great* (Boulder, Colo.: Jim Collins, 2005), 9–13.

11. Ibid., 11.

12. Jim Herrington, Mike Bonem, and James H. Furr, *Leading Congregational Change: A Practical Guide for the Transformational Journey* (San Francisco: Jossey-Bass, 2000), 16–27.

13. David Keirsey and Marilyn Bates, *Please Understand Me*, 3rd edition. (Del Mar, Calif.: Prometheus Nemesis Book Company, 1984).

Step 4

1. Hugh Mackay, "A Seasonal Promise of Renewal" (March 25, 2005). www.theage.com.au/news/hugh-mackay/a-seasonal-promise-of-renewal/2005/03/24/ 1111525286987.html. Accessed July 12, 2006.

2. David Roozen, cited in a handout distributed at the General Executive Council meeting of the American Baptist Churches USA, March 2006.

NOTES

3. Roy M. Oswald and Otto Kroeger, *Personality Type and Religious Leadership* (Washington, D.C.: The Alban Institute, 1988), 88.

4. Patrick Lencioni, *The Four Obsessions of an Extraordinary Executive: A Leadership Fable* (San Francisco: Jossey-Bass, 2000), 93–96.

5. Family Clusters are described in Margaret M. Sawin, *Family Enrichment with Family Clusters* (Valley Forge, Pa.: Judson, 1979).

Step 5

1. Ben Johnson, *95 Theses for the Church* (Decatur, Ga.: CTS Press, 1995), 27–28.

2. Richard J. Foster, *Celebration of Discipline: The Path to Spiritual Growth* (San Francisco: HarperSanFrancisco, 1978).

3. Henri J. M. Nouwen, *Reaching Out: The Three Movements of the Spiritual Life* (Garden City, N.Y.: Doubleday, 1975), 46–47, 51.

Step 6

1. Excerpted from Teresa of Avila, "Christ Has No Body but Yours" (1515–1582). www.journeywithjesus.net/PoemsAnd Prayers/Teresa_Of_Avila_Christ_ Has_No _Body.shtml. Accessed July 12, 2006.

Step 8

1. Quoted by Eugene H. Peterson, *A Long Obedience in the Same Direction: Discipleship in an Instant Society* (Downers Grove, Ill.: InterVarsity Press, 1980).

2. Everett M. Rogers, *Diffusion of Innovations,* 5th ed. (New York: The Free Press, 2003).

Step 9

1. Jimmy Carter, *Our Endangered Values: America's Moral Crisis* (New York: Simon and Schuster, 2005), 32–33.

2. Eileen W. Lindner, ed., *2006 Yearbook of American and Canadian Churches: Postmodern Christianity: Emergent Church and Blogs* (New York: National Council of Churches of Christ, 2006).

3. *Blog* is short for weblog, a journal or newsletter that is frequently updated by an individual or website for general public consumption. A *podcast* is an MP3 audio file that is available via a webfeed to online subscribers who can listen to the desired program at their leisure.

4. See note 4, Step 1.

5. One helpful and well-tested model, Natural Church Development, is described in Step 12, p. 129.

6. *2006 Planning Guide for Disciple-Making Congregations* (Valley Forge, Pa.: National Ministries, American Baptist Churches in the USA, 2006), 2–11. Used by permission. An expanded version of this guide is available on a CD from

Judson Resources at 800-4-JUDSON. The expanded version includes suggested resources and questions to consider.

Step 10

1. The foundational work for understanding the missional church comes from missiologist Lesslie Newbigin. A basic textbook from the Gospel and Our Culture Network is Darrell L. Guder, ed., *Missional Church: A Vision for the Sending of the Church in North America* (Grand Rapids: Eerdmans, 1998). Three recent books that would be grist for discussion about becoming a missional church are Reggie McNeal, *The Present Future: Six Tough Questions for the Church* (San Francisco: Jossey-Bass, 2003); Robert Lewis and Wayne Cordeiro, *Culture Shift: Transforming Your Church from the Inside Out* (San Francisco: Jossey-Bass, 2005); and Michael Frost and Alan Hirsch, *The Shaping of Things to Come: Innovation and Mission for the 21st-Century Church* (Peabody, Mass.: Hendrickson, 2003).

2. To learn more about emotional intelligence and leadership, I recommend Daniel Goleman, Richard Boyatzis, and Annie McKee, *Primal Leadership: Realizing the Power of Emotional Intelligence* (Boston: Harvard Business School Press, 2002).

3. I used the ECI360 from Hay-McBer Associates.

Step 11

1. Steve Nicholson and Jeff Bailey, *Coaching Church Planters: A Manual for Church Planters and Those Who Coach Them* (Stafford, Tex.: Association of Vineyard Churches, 2001), 7.

2. Stephen C. Lundin, Harry Paul, and John Christensen, *FISH! with DVD: A Remarkable Way to Boost Morale and Improve Results* (New York: Hyperion, 2000); Stephen C. Lundin, John Christensen, and Harry Paul, *FISH! Sticks: A Remarkable Way to Adapt to Changing Times and Keep Your Work Fresh* (New York: Hyperion, 2003). All of the *FISH!* resources can be found at www.charthouse.com.

3. For more information about group stages, I recommend Susan A. Wheelan, *Creating Effective Teams: A Guide for Members and Leaders* (Thousand Oaks, Calif.: SAGE, 1999), 25–30.

4. George W. Bullard Jr., *Pursuing the Full Kingdom Potential of Your Congregation* (St. Louis: Lake Hickory Resources, 2005), 203–4.

5. Daniel Goleman, Richard Boyatzis, and Annie McKee, *Primal Leadership: Realizing the Power of Emotional Intelligence* (Boston: Harvard Business School Press, 2002), 59–63.

6. Nicholson and Bailey, 27–34.

7. G. H. C. Macgregor, "The Acts of the Apostles," *The Interpreter's Bible*, vol. 9 (Nashville: Abingdon, 1954), 68.

8. Thomas G. Bandy, *Coaching Change: Breaking Down Resistance, Building Up Hope* (Nashville: Abingdon, 2000), 25.

Step 12

1. Harry Emerson Fosdick, *The Meaning of Prayer* (Nashville: Abingdon, 1915), 65.

2. Brad Abare and Kevin D. Hendricks, *Ministries Today*, "Marketing Your Church without Diluting Your Message" (Lake Mary, Fla.: Strang Communications, 2005), 1–4 website.

3. Jackson Carroll, quoted in G. Jeffrey MacDonald, "Churches Seeking Marketing-savvy Breed of Pastor," *Christian Science Monitor* (August 19, 2005). www.csmonitor.com/2005/0819/ p01s03-ussc.html. Accessed July 11, 2006.

4. George H. Martin, *Advertising the Local Church* (Winsted, Minn.: Church Ad Project, 1984).

5. Kimberly Pace, M. Garlinda Burton, et al., *Speaking Faith: The Essential Handbook for Religion Communication,* 7th ed. (New York: Religious Communications Council, 2005).

6. The original article by George W. Bullard Jr. appeared in *NET Results*, September 2001.

7. The four studies and links are *Faith Communities Today* (http://fact.hartsem.edu/researchfindings.htm), *Organizing Religious Work Study* (http://hirr.hartsem.edu/about/about_ or w_cong-report.html), *National Congregations Study* (http://s6.library.arizona.edu/natcong/), *U.S. Congregational Life Survey* (www.uscongregations.org/keycong.htm).

8. Nancy T. Ammerman, Jackson W. Carroll, Carl S. Dudley, and William McKinney, *Studying Congregations: A New Handbook* (Nashville: Abingdon, 1998).

9. Christian A. Schwartz, *Natural Church Development: A Guide to Eight Essential Qualities of Healthy Churches* (St. Charles. Ill.: ChurchSmart Resources, 1996), and Christian A. Schwartz and Christoph Schalk, *Implementation Guide to Natural Church Development* (Carol Stream, Ill.: ChurchSmart Resources, 1998).

10. For more information about Natural Church Planting, contact Phillip Alessi at CRM—Natural Church Planting and Multiplication, cell 917-399-5094, e-mail palessi69aol.com, or visit www.youresource.com/natural_church_plant _development1.htm.